THE COMPLETE GUIDE
TO MANAGING
A PORTFOLIO
OF MUTUAL FUNDS

D0068657

THE COMPLETE GUIDE
TO MANAGING
A PORTFOLIO
OF MUTUAL FUNDS

RONALD K. RUTHERFORD, CFP, CIMA

**The McGraw-Hill/IAFP Series in
Financial Planning**

INTERNATIONAL ASSOCIATION
FOR FINANCIAL PLANNING

McGraw-Hill

New York   San Francisco   Washington, D.C.   Auckland   Bogotá
Caracas   Lisbon   London   Madrid   Mexico City   Milan
Montreal   New Delhi   San Juan   Singapore
Sydney   Tokyo   Toronto

Library of Congress Cataloging-in-Publication Data

Rutherford, Ronald K.
    The complete guide to managing a portfolio of mutual funds / by
Ronald K. Rutherford.
        p.   cm.
    ISBN 0-7863-1138-X
    1. Mutual funds. 2. Portfolio management. I. Title.
HG4530.R88   1997
332.63'27—dc21   97-36926
                                                                    CIP

McGraw-Hill
A Division of The McGraw-Hill Companies

  2 3 4 5 6 7 8 9 0   DOC/DOC   9 0 3 2 1 0 9 8

ISBN 0-7863-1138-X

*The sponsoring editor for this book was Stephen Isaacs, the editing
supervisor was Curt Berkowitz, and the production supervisor was
Suzanne W. B. Rapcavage. It was set in Palatino by Terry Leaden of
McGraw-Hill's Professional Book Group composition unit.*

Printed and bound by R. R. Donnelley & Sons Company.

This publication is designed to provide accurate and authoritative
information in regard to the subject matter covered. It is sold with
the understanding that neither the author nor the publisher is
engaged in rendering legal, accounting, or other professional
service. If legal advice or other expert assistance is required, the
services of a competent professional person should be sought.
—From a Declaration of Principles jointly adopted by a Committee of
  the American Bar Association and a Committee of Publishers.

This book is printed on recycled, acid-free paper containing
a minimum of 50% recycled, de-inked fiber.

DEDICATION

Part-time authors like me must extract writing time from what passes for "normal" activities. That time must come from the business, from family activities, or both. Most important, authors need time to think through what they want to say. They also need time to research, to write the manuscript, to create illustrations, and to discuss their work with those involved in the process. I developed a schedule with milestones, but the project still took longer and more effort than I initially envisioned.

My spouse, Suzzette, is the person who endured the most hassles during this process. Fortunately, she had the vision, maturity, and understanding to persevere. She helped me keep the needle on the stress meter out of the red zone.

I am also indebted to my business partner, Suzzette. Yes, she is the same person I mentioned in the preceding paragraph. I performed some of the duties of authorship during business hours—there were times when I had no choice. That made Suzzette's client activities and workload go from a reading of "heavy" to "you are pushing it" on the Richter scale.

In addition to pulling up the slack in the office, she found the time to read the early drafts of the manuscript and make constructive suggestions. Her perspective was not only as a CFP but also as an attorney. In that sense, she acted as my in-house counsel.

In short, Suzzette made the difference.

This dedication would be incomplete without also thanking my Mother. From her home in Texas, she took on the responsibility of making regular imaginary trips to the wall of worry on behalf of Suzzette and me. We got many questions from her. "Are you getting enough sleep?" "Are you maintaining a properly balanced diet?" "Are you taking time to relax?" This noble undertaking relieved Suzzette and me of the burden of having to worry about these matters ourselves. As a public service, Mother can give you directions to the wall if you cannot find it by yourself. She asked me to make something clear. She lacks the shelf space to take on any more worries or wall climbing.

C O N T E N T S

PREFACE

When the publisher first approached me about this book, I was flattered. They asked me to write as much as I was willing to disclose about my experience in designing and managing portfolios for clients. We make use of both mutual funds and individual securities, the choice depending on client preferences. We also have both institutional and individual private clients. The publisher asked me to focus this book on mutual funds and on individual private clients.

Then the weight of it all settled in. It took me several months to think through what I wanted to say. When I finally started the writing, it went smoothly. Now that I have recovered from my initial doubts, I feel good about the result. The real test, however, is if you feel the same way after reading it. More to the point, I will have succeeded if you get a few good ideas that you can use in your practice to make your client portfolios better. I also assume that many individual investors ready for the next level of sophistication can find useful information here.

This book is about clients and how we, as advisors, can best serve them. We have a duty to our clients to make the best use of their assets within the context of their goals and risk preferences. For the core part of the client portfolio, the design should produce the target rate of return with the least amount of risk. As advisors, you and I need to articu-

late an *investment philosophy* that is the foundation of everything we do as advisors. Next, we should be able to describe
a *process* that we use to design a portfolio and to select and
monitor mutual fund managers. This book helps to meet
that need.

All of this is written in the context of an Investment
Policy Statement (IPS). Why is an IPS so important?
Consider the analogy of a flight plan. Many things may
happen to throw a plane off course. It could be mechanical
failure, bad weather, improper communication or execution
of air traffic control instructions, evasive action to avoid
another aircraft, or pilot error. An IPS is like a flight plan. It
helps us get back on course. It helps everyone involved to
keep their eyes on the ball. The focal point for the IPS is the
target rate of return required to achieve specific client goals.

It helps to begin at the beginning—that is, you should
have a clear understanding of the investment categories
and the weighting of those categories that are suitable for
your client. Included here are examples using the traditional mean-variance approach first introduced by
Markowitz and later enhanced by Sharpe. In addition, there
are illustrations of the benchmark and the below-target-risk
methods of design. Some boldly proclaim the below-target-
risk method as post-Modern Portfolio Theory (MPT). While
that may be a bit presumptuous, I find the method power-
ful. I also find that clients have a much easier time understanding it versus the traditional MPT approach.

Next, we come to the age-old debate about passive
versus active investors. The word *passive* suggests a strict
buy-and-hold approach. In reality, even index funds have a
certain amount of turnover. The real issue is return after
expenses and after taxes if applicable. Many active managers are closer to this real-world definition of *passive investing* than to active, hot-fund aggressive investing strategies.

They are long-term investors. You can start with Warren Buffett. Some mutual fund managers also have low expenses and low turnover. Many people equate index funds with low expenses. A closer inspection shows that this is not always the case. To blindly buy any index fund without checking these details can be a serious breach of our duty to our clients.

How do we select active managers? Critical to this process is the proper characterization of the style of the manager. One important approach is the *portfolio method*, which is the traditional approach of evaluating the portfolio holdings of a fund. This is vital input to the selection decision. Another relatively new technique is the *returns method*. After several months of testing, I find that this method is useful as a *supporting tool*. If there is divergence between the two methods, I probe deeper to find the reason. I particularly favor a calculation that makes use of a 6-month look-back period resulting from a rolling 12-month average of returns. This puts the aging of the results in the same period as the portfolio method. Traditional returns-based style analysis makes use of rolling 36-month returns. That results in a look-back period of 18 months. One comedian in the crowd suggests that, after 18 months, our clothes would be out of style.

Here are some additional points discussed in this book in the context of manager selection. These things seem to matter:

- ◆ Consistency of returns
- ◆ Long-term record of accomplishment
- ◆ Expenses and turnover
- ◆ Tax efficiency
- ◆ Diversification
- ◆ Anomalies in portfolio composition

ACKNOWLEDGMENTS

This book is a product of the willingness of many organizations within the financial services industry to contribute their time and the use of their products.

First, I want to thank two people at Frontier Analytics, Inc.: Randal J. Moore, President, and Kamaryn T. Tanner, Vice President, Product Development. Ms. Tanner helped in the interpretation of the results from their portfolio design product known as *Investment Plus*. Specifically it included optimization models covering the (1) mean variance, (2) benchmark, and (3) below-target-risk methods. It also covered style analysis using the returns method. Mr. Moore helped with guidance and introductions about the many asset class indices used in this book.

Second, I want to thank the people at Morningstar. Don Phillips, President, spent a great deal of time with me to discuss his perspective about the truths and myths that make up the body of knowledge about mutual funds. His staff also provided me with an advanced copy of *Principia Plus* with *Advanced Analytics*. This allowed me to get an early start on learning its new functions. I also made regular telephone calls to the people in the Morningstar support staff to discuss the use and interpretation of the results from *Principia Plus*.

Mr. Moore at Frontier Analytics, Inc., and Mr. Phillips at Morningstar granted me permission to use many of the 120 illustrations found here. By quickly paging through this book, you can tell that I strongly believe in the power of illustrations to reinforce a strategy or summarize a statistical study.

Next, I must mention Evelyn L. Brust, Executive Director of the Investment Management Consultants Association (IMCA). Evelyn gave me permission to reproduce the IMCA guidelines for an institutional-level Investment Policy Statement.

Others within the industry offered advice and support. One is Dr. Frank Sortino, Director of the Pension Research Institute and professor emeritus of finance at San Francisco State University. Dr. Sortino is a leading advocate of the use of downside risk as a focal point in portfolio design. Another supporter was Donald Trone, who is the founder and executive director of the Investment Management Council, a division of Callan Associates, Inc. He contributed encouragement and ideas throughout the process.

In addition, I wish to acknowledge the contribution of the many prestigious firms that granted the use of their indices and other data for this book:

- American Stock Exchange, Inc.
- BARRA
- Dimensional Fund Advisors
- Frank Russell Company
- Merrill Lynch
- Morgan Stanley Capital International

- National Association of Real Estate Investment Trusts
- Salomon Brothers, Inc.
- Standard and Poor's
- ValueLine, Inc.
- Wilshire Associates, Inc.

THE COMPLETE GUIDE
TO MANAGING
A PORTFOLIO
OF MUTUAL FUNDS

CHAPTER 1

Setting Investment Policy

A PROFILE OF OUR CLIENTS

This book is about clients. It is a view from the bridge of a practitioner. It documents a response to client needs and perspectives. Our clients are both individuals and institutions, the institutions consisting of retirement plans and endowment funds. The focus of this book is on individuals. In some cases, individual clients have assets they have accumulated. In other cases, they are the beneficiaries of inherited wealth. Typically our clients are successful in their chosen field. Some still work and others are in retirement. I see about as many paths to wealth accumulation as there are clients. The source of accumulated wealth can be earnings from a closely held business, from a professional practice, or from a corporate setting. Figure 1–1 shows a distribution of our clients by major category. Figure 1–2 shows a breakout by those retired versus those still working.

Most of our individual clients are affluent. I refer to them as "private clients." They typically have the intellect

FIGURE 1–1

Practice Profile: Private Client Categories

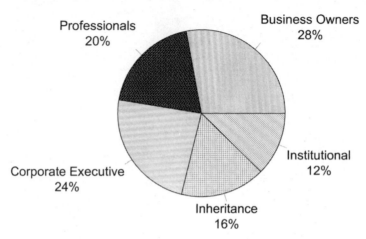

Professionals
20%

Business Owners
28%

Institutional
12%

Inheritance
16%

Corporate Executive
24%

Source: Rutherford Asset Planning, Inc.

FIGURE 1–2

Practice Profile: Private Clients Still Working
versus Retired

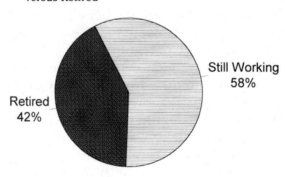

Still Working
58%

Retired
42%

Source: Rutherford Asset Planning, Inc.

to design and manage their portfolio. They come to us because they lack the skills, the time, or the inclination to deal with the details. They recognize that their financial assets represent the fuel for the engine of both day-to-day living and the fulfillment of long-term aspirations. They are mature enough to know that successful investing requires specialized skills, as well as a discipline and objectivity about investments, that they typically do not possess.

I help my clients to design, execute, track, and update their investment portfolios. The process is a continuous one. The design is at the asset class level. In some cases, I implement the design with individual securities and direct investments; in other cases, I select and monitor mutual fund managers. The focus of this book is on the use of mutual funds, either actively managed or indexed or a combination of those.

OVERVIEW OF THIS BOOK

Let us do a fast-forward through what you are about to read so that you can see each chapter in the context of the whole book. My goal here is to establish a broad framework upon which to build.

Chapters 1 and 2 emphasize strategic planning. I cannot stress enough the importance of a tailored, long-term financial strategy for your clients. This includes the definition and quantification of their goals. It results in the calculation of the annual target rate of return required for achievement of these goals. The tangible manifestation of the strategy is a documented blueprint called the *Investment Policy Statement* (IPS). This blueprint becomes the focal point for strategic and tactical decisions about the clients' portfolio. This is especially critical at crunch time when an asset class heads south. Without an IPS, it is easy to fall into the trap of doing something precipitous as the tide goes out and the music stops.

In the corporate world, strategic plans are typically refreshed every year. In a former life, I was part of that process. The IPS should likewise have an annual refresh. The refresh incorporates changes in assumptions or circumstances. Examples include changes in client goals, the resources available to fund those goals, assumptions for inflation, and the suppositions about the characteristics of investment categories going forward. Chapter 2 includes an outline of an IPS, courtesy of the Investment Management Consultants Association, which I use to illustrate how this format can be adapted for individual investors.

The focus of *Chapters 3 and 4* is asset class investing. After a tribute to some of the giants of portfolio theory, I go on to discuss not only Modern Portfolio Theory but also other important theories that followed. There are illustrations of portfolio design. The first makes use of the mean-variance approach developed by Dr. Harry Markowitz. There is also a discussion of the Capital Asset Pricing Model developed by Dr. William Sharpe. Other giants of portfolio theory discussed here are Stephen Ross who conceived the Arbitrage Pricing Theory and Barr Rosenberg who constructed a model of covariance that includes industry factors. There are illustrations of other methods as well, including *benchmark optimization* and *below target risk*. Another name for this method is *downside risk.* The downside risk concept embodies the notion of *minimum acceptable return* (MAR). Dr. Frank Sortino is closely identified with the development of this idea. Some advisors may feel more comfortable communicating the downside risk concept to clients than the traditional Mean-Variance Optimization from Modern Portfolio Theory (MPT). The downside risk concept has an appealing sound, look, and feel that is not as apparent in MPT. I find that clients often have an easier time relating the notion of downside risk and minimum acceptable return to their circumstances.

Chapters 5 and 6 are about the importance of buy-and-hold, passive investing. One type of mutual fund applicable to this concept is the index fund. Index funds, especially those with exposure to the large stocks represented by the Standard and Poor's 500 Stock Index, are in vogue today. Over the last few years, they have outperformed the vast majority of actively managed funds. That was not always the case. Dogmatic use of a pure index fund implementation may not be in the best interests of the client. The issue is not index funds versus actively managed funds. Rather, the issue is cost, turnover, and taxes. Actively managed funds with low cost and low turnover are more likely to outperform index funds than those with high cost and high turnover. Further, not all index funds are equal. Some have relatively high costs, mediocre performance, or both. A passive strategy emphasizing low cost and low turnover funds is a viable strategy. That strategy may include index funds, actively managed funds, or a combination. This, for instance, can become the primary part of a portfolio design based on a core-plus-satellite approach.

Chapters 7 and 8 are about active investing and the selection of active managers. It begins with a tribute to active managers. Some are already legends; others are candidates for my Investors Hall of Fame. I then cover critical measurements for review by the advisor. Any good mutual fund manager should pass these hurdles with a comfortable margin of safety. How do you assign an active manager to an asset class or style? I do it with a pragmatic, two-pronged approach that elevates substance over form. I use *both* the portfolio method and the returns method. As I see it, they are *not* mutually exclusive. They are tools that call for confirmation. When I find divergence, it is a flag to dig deeper to find the reason for the divergence. The returns method described here has important adaptations that I find to be useful and productive at the practitioner level. Included is a case study for an equity fund and one for a bond fund.

My goal is a modest one. I hope that you get at least three or four good ideas that you can immediately use in your practice. These are ideas that have the potential to improve the productivity of the portfolios of your clients. This book is about what works for my clients and me. You have the luxury to choose those ideas that make sense for you and your clients.

One final point about the format of this book. I had the option to provide many pages of detailed mathematical formulas and definitions. I chose not to do that; instead, I provided footnotes with references that satisfy that need for those of you who have the curiosity and inclination to dig deeper. My preference is that you perceive this as a practitioner's handbook, not a college textbook. Enough, already! Let us get on with it!

FOUNDATION OF STRATEGIC PLANNING

Successful investing starts with strategic planning. Listen to what one noted author says about strategic planning. Here is a conversation between two of his characters:

> *Character 1:* "Would you tell me, please, which way I ought to go from here?"
>
> *Character 2:* "That depends a good deal on where you want to get to."
>
> *Character 1:* "I don't much care where."

Character 2: "Then it doesn't matter which way you go."

Character 1: "So long as I get somewhere?"

Character 2: "Oh, you're sure to do that, if you only walk long enough."

You probably recognize that bit of wisdom. It is from Lewis Carroll's *Alice's Adventures in Wonderland*. Did his words set the wheels in motion for the rise of strategic planning? That is doubtful. But the words do have profound if unintended implications for planning. Simply put, *strategic planning* is the process for defining, prioritizing, and documenting goals together with the chosen path to reach those goals. The plan includes analysis of the best, worst, and most likely cases. A corporation typically develops a strategic plan for the upcoming 5-year period. Each year they develop a new 5-year plan starting from the new fiscal year, using a few basic steps.

> Simply put, *strategic planning* is the process for defining, prioritizing, and documenting goals together with the chosen path to reach those goals.

First, they define the size and growth rate of their target market or markets. Next, they choose their objective for the share their company will hold in that market. Next, they carve out the after-tax profit that they want. The difference between the revenue and the profit objectives gives them expense targets. It is at this point in the process that the fun part begins. They frequently have more than one product group that feels that it has the best chance to reach that market. Each of these product groups depends on support from other divisions to achieve their plan. As one might expect, there is always more demand for support resources within the company than there are resources available. *Support resources* as used here include such areas as component supply, manufacturing capacity, and staff to sell and service the products. The planners must then prioritize. Each product group competes for the scarce resources. If the groups do not agree on a solution, they escalate up the organization chart until no issues remain. This *contention process* produces a plan with the most productive deployment of limited assets. It is the highest and best use of the company resources.

This general planning concept makes a great deal of sense for clients in setting a strategy for their investments. Many who come to us freely admit that they do not have a clear idea of where they want to go. Those few that have thought through their goals do not know the best way to get there. Thus, I must work with the client to develop a strategic plan for client investments using an established discipline that has the most likelihood for success.

The Investment Policy Statement

The *Investment Policy Statement* (IPS) is a documented strategy for fulfillment of client investment goals. It serves two purposes. First, it is a *decision-making aid*. Clients, working with the advisor, use it as a reference point for making both short-term, operational decisions and for long-term, strategic decisions regarding their investments. Second, the IPS is a *tool for communication* between parties. The IPS provides the historic record of the strategy and the underlying rationale.

Let me put it in perspective. You can think of an Investment Policy Statement as a game plan for a coach, a flight plan for a pilot, a blueprint for a building contractor, a musical score for a conductor, or a business plan for an owner. There is

> You can think of an Investment Policy Statement as a game plan for a coach, a flight plan for a pilot, a blueprint for a building contractor, a musical score for a conductor, or a business plan for an owner.

a common thread, made of two intertwined strands, that weaves its way through all these documents. One strand is a strategy, and the other is a plan of action for achieving the goals of the strategy.

WHAT DOES THE IPS CONTAIN?

Let us first consider the baseline format for an Investment Policy Statement that is recommended by the Investment Management Consultants Association (IMCA) and that is presented in the box that follows. IMCA is an association of professionals who provide support and advice to investment committees and retirement plan sponsors. The client is the large institutional investor whose primary responsibility consists mostly of public- and private-sector retirement plans. Other institutions that might use this plan are foundations and endowment funds. After the presentation of the institutional format are some of my suggestions for adapting it for the private client.

FORMALIZING INVESTMENT POLICY

"The Investment Policy Statement is a formal document outlining the objectives, goals, and guidelines for a fund; its purpose is to (1) establish a clear understanding between the decision makers for the fund and any investment managers employed to manage fund assets; (2) to provide guidance and limitations in the investment of fund assets; and (3) to provide a meaningful basis for the evaluation of fund and manager performance.

Moreover, the establishment of written investment objectives and goals for qualified plans is suggested by the

Source: "Investment Planning and Policy," published by the Investment Management Consultants Association, Denver, CO, pp. 21–28.

FORMALIZING INVESTMENT POLICY Continued

Employee Retirement Income Security Act of 1974 (ERISA) under Sections 402(a)(1), 402(b)(l), and 402(b)(2). The Act states that every employee benefit plan must 'provide a procedure for establishing and carrying out a funding policy in a method consistent with the objectives of the plan' (ERISA 402(b)(1)). This provision certainly points to the need for an investment policy. A formal investment policy for other investors is desirable and prudent also.

A well-constructed Investment Policy Statement should be drawn up for every investing entity, individual or institutional, and should contain the following elements:

- Statement of Purpose
- Statement of Responsibilities
- Investment Objectives and Goals
- Investment Guidelines
- Investment Performance Review and Evaluation
- Communications

Statement of Purpose provides background information relating to the plan and the sponsoring organization, including name and type of plan, the purpose for which it was established, and participant demographics. Factors relating to the sponsor which may have an impact on the plan's viability may be included, such as the organization's industry, profitability, and sensitivity to the economic and business cycle. In addition, specific needs or characteristics of the plan should be included such as the source(s) of contributions.

For example, the Statement of Purpose for a corporate defined benefit plan may begin as follows:

'The Retirement Plan for Employees of XYZ Company' (hereinafter

Source: "Investment Planning and Policy," published by the Investment Management Consultants Association, Denver, CO, pp. 21–28.

FORMALIZING INVESTMENT POLICY Continued

referred to as 'the Plan') was established to provide pension and retirement benefits for employees participating in the Plan. It is a noncontributory defined benefit plan where contributions are determined by the Plan's actuary and made by the Company only (i.e., no employee contributions) annually.

Statement of Responsibilities identifies the parties associated with the fund and the functions, responsibilities, and activities of each with respect to the management of fund assets. Parties include (but are not limited to):

◆ Fiduciaries who are ultimately responsible for the Plan, the appropriateness of its investment policy, and execution. They may include the Board of Trustees, Administrative Committee, or Investment Policy Committee.

◆ Investment Manager(s) with responsibility for day-to-day investment management of plan assets, including specific security selection and the timing of purchases and sales.

◆ Master Custodian with responsibility for safekeeping securities, collections and disbursements, and periodic accounting statements.

◆ Investment Consultant with responsibility for assisting the plan sponsor in developing investment policy and objectives and for monitoring performance of the Plan and its investment managers.

Investment Objectives describe the plan sponsor's return expectations, sensitivity to risk, and time horizon. Investment objectives and goals should be realistic and appropriate given fund needs.

Sample investment objectives are outlined below:

Source: "Investment Planning and Policy," published by the Investment Management Consultants Association, Denver, CO, pp. 21–28.

FORMALIZING INVESTMENT POLICY Continued

- *Minimize Short-Term Risk:*   The likelihood of sharp declines in asset value in any one year should be minimized. The possibility of a moderate decline in asset value is a risk the Trustees accept in order to achieve long-term growth; however, negative returns in any one year are not allowed.

- *Preservation of Capital:*   Preservation of invested capital is a principal objective, and the fund should earn at least a positive return over the investment time horizon. Capital gains, once earned, are to be protected.

- *Preservation of Purchasing Power:*   Asset growth, exclusive of contributions and withdrawals, should exceed the rate of inflation in order to preserve purchasing power of fund assets.

- *Long-Term Growth of Capital:*   The asset value of the fund, exclusive of contributions or withdrawals, should grow in the long run and earn through a combination of investment income and capital appreciation a rate of return in excess of a balanced market index while incurring less risk than such index. It is recognized that short-term fluctuations in the capital markets may result in the loss of capital on occasion (i.e., negative rates of return).

- *Stability of Returns:*   While some risk is warranted in pursuing long-term growth of capital, consistent annual returns with low volatility in investment performance are very desirable.

- *Aggressive Growth of Capital:*   The fund's objective is to maximize returns through capital appreciation, and to a lesser extent, investment income.

Source: "Investment Planning and Policy," published by the Investment Management Consultants Association, Denver, CO, pp. 21–28.

FORMALIZING INVESTMENT POLICY Continued

◆ *Current Income:* Generate a level of current income sufficient to meet withdrawal needs. Any shortfall in current income required to meet spending needs will be provided by capital appreciation.

Investment Goals are specific numeric targets by which we measure whether or not objectives have been met. They may be expressed as an absolute return target, relative to a market index, or a minimum required dollar amount or income yield. Sample investment goals are outlined below:

◆ To meet or exceed the rate of return of a balanced market index comprised of the S&P 500 stock index, Lehman Government/Corporate bond index, and U.S. Treasury Bills in similar proportion to the Asset Allocation Policy of the fund.

◆ To generate a total rate of return (investment income plus capital appreciation) of at least 9%.

◆ To meet or exceed the risk-free rate of return (as represented by U.S. Treasury Bills).

◆ To generate a current income return at a rate which allows the Trustees to withdraw $10,000 annually.

◆ To earn at least a 2.0% annualized rate of return on a risk-adjusted basis.

◆ To meet or exceed the inflation rate (as measured by the Consumer Price Index) by 300 basis points per year on average.

◆ To match or exceed the actuarial rate of interest of 8.5% per year on average.

Investment Guidelines are the framework within which investments are made. These guidelines may contain lan-

Source: "Investment Planning and Policy," published by the Investment Management Consultants Association, Denver, CO, pp. 21–28.

FORMALIZING INVESTMENT POLICY Continued

guage pertaining to issues such as proxy voting, liquidity needs, trading and execution guidelines or social responsibility in investing. For example,

◆ [*For Corporate or Taft-Hartley Plan*] *ERISA Standards:* Investments should be selected and managed in accordance with the fiduciary standards of ERISA; that is (a) in the sole interest of Plan participants and beneficiaries; (b) with the care, skill, prudence and diligence under the circumstances then prevailing that a prudent man acting in a like capacity and familiar with such matters would use in the conduct of an enterprise of a like character and of like aims; and (c) by diversifying the investment so as to minimize the risk of large losses.

◆ [*For Public Fund, Endowment, Foundation; Individual Investor*] *Prudent Man Rule:* Investments are to be made consistent with the safeguards and diversity to which a prudent investor would adhere, i.e., exercising judgment and care, under the circumstances prevailing, which men of ordinary prudence would employ in the management of their own affairs . . . not in regard to speculation, but to the permanent disposition of their funds, considering both income and safety of capital.

◆ *Liquidity:* The Plan's cash flow will be monitored on a regular basis by the Trustees, and sufficient liquidity should be maintained to fund benefit payment outflows. When withdrawals become necessary, the Trustees will notify the Investment Manager(s) as far in advance as possible to allow them sufficient time to build up necessary liquid reserves. The Investment Manager(s) will be expected to review the cash flow requirements with the Trustees at least annually.

Source: "Investment Planning and Policy," published by the Investment Management Consultants Association, Denver, CO, pp. 21–28.

FORMALIZING INVESTMENT POLICY Continued

◆ *Volatility:* Consistent with the desire for adequate diversification, Investment Policy for the Plan is based on the assumption that the volatility of the portfolio will be similar to that of the market. Consequently, it is expected that the volatility of the total portfolio, in aggregate, will be reasonably close to the volatility of a balanced market index weighted to match the actual asset mix of the Plan.

◆ *Proxy Voting Policy:* The Investment Manager(s) shall have the sole and exclusive right to vote any and all proxies solicited in connection with securities held by the Plan. The Investment Manager(s) shall furnish the Trustees with any written proxy voting policy statement, and shall keep records with respect to its voting decisions and submit a report on request to the Trustees summarizing votes cast.

◆ *Trading and Execution Guidelines:* The Investment Manager(s) shall have the discretion to execute securities transactions with brokerage firms of their choosing; however, this selection shall be based on the quality of execution rendered, the value of research information provided, the financial health and integrity of the brokerage firm, and the overall efficiency in transacting business.

   Ultimately, however, the Trustees retain the right to direct brokerage commissions subject to best execution. When the Investment Manager(s) directs commissions on behalf of the Trustees and Plan, the direction will be contingent upon the institution being competitive in both price and execution for the specific transaction.

Source: "Investment Planning and Policy," published by the Investment Management Consultants Association, Denver, CO, pp. 21–28.

FORMALIZING INVESTMENT POLICY Continued

◆ *Social Responsibility:*   No assets shall be invested in securities of any organization that does not meet the standard for socially and morally responsible investments established by the Trustees and communicated separately in writing to the Investment Manager.

Asset Mix Guidelines identify asset classes approved for investment with the maximum and minimum range for each asset category. For example:

It shall be the policy of the Plan to invest the assets in accordance with the maximum and minimum range for each asset category as stated below:

Asset Category	Policy	Minimum	Maximum
Common Stocks	%	%	%
Fixed Income	%	%	%
Short-Term Investments	%	%	%
International Investments	%	%	%
Real Estate	%	%	%
Other assets	%	%	%

The Asset Mix Policy and acceptable *minimum* and maximum ranges established by the Trustees represent a long-term view. As such, rapid and significant market movements may cause the Plan's actual asset mix to fall outside the policy range, but any divergence should be of a short-term nature.

Portfolio Limitations (such as quality ratings, diversification, and selection criteria) and restricted investments would be outlined in this section. For example,

Source: "Investment Planning and Policy," published by the Investment Management Consultants Association, Denver, CO, pp. 21–28.

FORMALIZING INVESTMENT POLICY Continued

Equities:

♦ *Types of Securities:*   Equity securities shall mean common stocks or equivalents (American Depository Receipts, etc. plus issues convertible into common stock), preferred stocks, and foreign stocks.

♦ *Diversification:*   The equity portfolio should be well diversified to avoid undue exposure to any single economic sector, industry group, or individual security.

♦ *Quality and Marketability:*   Common and convertible preferred stocks should be of good quality and listed on either the New York or American Stock Exchange or in the NASDAQ system with the requirement that such stocks have adequate market liquidity relative to the size of the investment.

♦ *Capitalization:*   Stocks must be those of corporations with market capitalization exceeding $250 million.

♦ *Concentration by Issuer:*   No more than 5% of the equity portfolio based on market value shall be invested in the securities of any one issuing corporation at the time of purchase.

No more than 20% of the equity portfolio based on market value should be invested in any one industry at the time of purchase.

Fixed Income Investments:

♦ *Types of Securities:*   Funds not invested in cash equivalents (securities maturing in one year or less) shall be invested entirely in marketable debt securities issued by either the United States Government, or agencies of

Source: "Investment Planning and Policy," published by the Investment Management Consultants Association, Denver, CO, pp. 21–28.

FORMALIZING INVESTMENT POLICY Continued

the United States Government, domestic corporations, including industrials and utilities, and domestic banks and other United States financial institutions.

◆ *Quality:*   Only fixed income securities that are rated AAA by Standard & Poor's or AAA by Moody's shall be purchased.

◆ *Maturity:*   The maturity of individual fixed income securities purchased in the portfolio will not exceed 12 years.

◆ *Restricted Investments:*   Categories of investments which are not eligible for investment without prior approval of the Trustees include:

1. Short sales
2. Margin purchases or other use of lending or borrowing of money
3. Private placements
4. Commodities
5. Foreign securities listed primarily outside the United States
6. American Depository Receipts (ADRs)
7. Security loans
8. Unregistered or restricted stock
9. Direct loans or extension lines of credit to any interested party
10. Warrants
11. Real estate mortgages
12. Options or futures

Source: "Investment Planning and Policy," published by the Investment Management Consultants Association, Denver, CO, pp. 21–28.

FORMALIZING INVESTMENT POLICY Continued

Investment Performance Review and Evaluation establishes the basis for measuring and evaluating fund and manager performance.

◆ Performance results for the Investment Manager(s) will be measured on a quarterly, semi-annual, and/or annual basis.

◆ Total fund performance will be measured against a balanced index composed of commonly accepted benchmarks weighted to match the long-term Asset Allocation Policy of the Plan.

◆ The investment performance of the total portfolio and equity and fixed income segments (both in terms of return and risk) will be measured against commonly accepted benchmarks.

◆ Total fund performance will be compared to a representative universe of professionally managed funds with the percentage of equity, fixed income, and cash equivalents to be indicative of the long-term Asset Allocation Policy of the Plan.

Communications is an integral part of the management process. This section addresses the need for regular and continued communications between the plan fiduciaries and investment managers by establishing the reporting requirements and the frequency of review meetings.

Communications with the Investment Consultant may be addressed in this section as well.

Investment Manager(s) Communications with the Trustees:

◆ Provide quarterly portfolio valuations and transaction listings.

Source: "Investment Planning and Policy," published by the Investment Management Consultants Association, Denver, CO, pp. 21–28.

FORMALIZING INVESTMENT POLICY Continued

- Meet at least [quarterly, semi-annually, annually] with the Trustees.

- Review past investment performance, evaluate the current investment outlook, and discuss investment strategy.

- Provide information regarding major changes in investment policy that may result in major investment strategy changes.

- Review any significant changes in management, research, personnel or ownership within the investment management firm.

- Other communications that the Investment Manager(s) feels are necessary to facilitate achievement of the Plan's objectives and goals.

- Forward to client and consultant SEC Form ADV, Parts I and II annually or at any interim point Form ADV is substantially revised.

- Manager will be available for telephone consultation on a reasonable basis.

Trustees' Communications With Consultant and Investment Manager(s):

- On a timely basis, provide revisions of the master Statement of Investment Policy, Objectives, and Guidelines.

- Meet at least [*quarterly, semi-annually, annually*] with the Investment Manager(s).

- Review and discuss any modifications and changes to the Plan's investment objectives, goals, and guidelines.

Source: "Investment Planning and Policy," published by the Investment Management Consultants Association, Denver, CO, pp. 21–28.

FORMALIZING INVESTMENT POLICY Concluded

- Identify any significant anticipated changes in the Plan's cash flow.

- Any other matters which may bear upon the Plan's assets.

SUMMARY

The depth or brevity of an Investment Policy Statement will vary from plan to plan. The language should provide meaningful guidance in the management of Plan assets but not be overly restrictive given changing economic, business, and investment market conditions. The Statement should be reviewed periodically and modifications made to reflect significant changes."

Source: "Investment Planning and Policy," published by the Investment Management Consultants Association, Denver, CO, pp. 21–28.

THE INVESTMENT POLICY STATEMENT—MODIFICATIONS FOR PRIVATE CLIENTS

The IPS guidelines published by IMCA are intended for large, institutional clients. These guidelines represent the collective wisdom and practical experience of the member consultants. Our focus here is on the Private Client, and the IMCA guidelines require a different viewpoint for this audience. Here is our view of the important modifications needed to tailor the IPS to the needs of the Private Client.

STATEMENT OF PURPOSE

This section lays the groundwork for the rest of the document. It first answers the question, "Who is the client?" It includes their name(s), address(es), birthday(s), and income tax brackets. Next, it describes the *broad aims* of the client. It documents the intended purpose of the financial assets considered in the portfolio design. The document contains the "as of" date of the IPS. Here is an example of wording:

> This Investment Policy Statement dated January 15, (Year), is for John and Mary Example. They live at 9 Yellow Brick Road in Their Town, Their State. John and Mary have birth dates of June 13, 1947, and October 2, 1948, respectively. The table below lists the income tax brackets of the Examples.

Tax Entity	Income Tax Bracket	Capital Gains Tax Bracket
Federal	39.6%	20%
State	9	9
Local	3	3

The overall aim of this portfolio design is to provide the funding for specific goals of the Examples. The definition of these goals is in the section of this document labeled "Investment Objectives."

STATEMENT OF RESPONSIBILITIES

This section describes the related parties involved in the IPS design and implementation process. It includes the investment advisor and the custodian. It *may* also include others such as a co-trustee, an auditor of the records, and those rendering tax and legal advice about the IPS. Here is an example of wording:

> The investment advisor is Rutherford Asset Planning, Inc. (RAP). Their headquarters location is 885 Third Avenue, Suite 2900, New York, NY 10022. The telephone number is

(212) 829-5580. The principal person responsible for your account is Ronald K. Rutherford. The custodian for the financial assets in your portfolio is XYZ Broker. RAP has a Limited Power of Attorney over your financial assets held with this custodian. This Limited Power of Attorney grants RAP the authority to direct trades on a discretionary basis and to receive duplicate records in both electronic and hard-copy form. It allows RAP to deal with the custodian in your behalf. The Limited Power of Attorney does *not* grant to RAP the authority to withdraw assets from your account.

An explanation to the reader seems appropriate here. Institutional clients are often immense in terms of the dollar amounts of assets under management. The investment committee of these entities typically hires an investment consultant. This consultant guides the committee through the process of portfolio design. They help the committee in the fulfillment of their fiduciary duty to act with the same care as would a "prudent investor." They assist the committee in the selection and ongoing oversight of money managers.[1] They also assist the committee to replace a manager if that becomes necessary.

Private clients typically do not have the massive financial resources of institutional clients, which makes it more difficult to use money managers. Money managers have a minimum amount they accept, and that amount is often beyond the reach of the Private Client. This is especially the case in the context of a portfolio with a variety of investment categories or asset classes. Each asset class typically requires a different money manager. Say, for example, that

---

1. Money managers select individual stocks and bonds. Their clients are usually institutional. The minimum amounts they accept are typically in the high six figures. Some have minimums in seven figures.

the portfolio design calls for eight separate asset classes. Let us assume that the money managers in the final list have $1 million minimums. That means $8 million for the portfolio. Minimums of $500,000 still call for a portfolio of $4 million. My wish is that all of your clients have $8 million and certainly at least $4 million to manage! If this is not the case, read more.

The point is, the advisor using mutual funds for implementation is not a money manager in the classic sense. The role of the advisor in working with the Private Client is more like that of the investment consultant than that of the money manager. There is selection of mutual fund managers to execute the portfolio design. The advisor oversees these managers and replaces them when and if that becomes necessary. The advisor reports to the client the periodic and long-term results of the mutual fund managers represented in the portfolio.

If the strategy calls for the use of index funds, there is still an important role for the advisor. First, there remains a need to provide advice about asset allocation going forward. Second, the large capitalization stock asset class has many index funds from which to choose. This is not the case for other asset classes. As we will see later, there are not very many pure index funds out there. Many index fund managers attempt to add value to the process. They do this in a variety of ways. One index fund manager told me privately that he "tweaks the portfolio."[2]

---

2. *Tweaking* is a highly technical term that is beyond the scope of this book.

INVESTMENT OBJECTIVES

This portion of the IPS is devoted to definitions of client risk tolerance and investment suitability. Advisors are fiduciaries. One responsibility they have is to tailor the portfolio so that it is appropriate for each client. "Cookie-cutter" or "one-size-fits-all" approaches are not appropriate. This is part of the process of "due diligence" about client needs and preferences. Most forms of risk tolerance and investment suitability questionnaires are *subjective* by nature. To my knowledge, there is no scientific, reproducible link between the results of these questionnaires and the success of the portfolio. The danger here is that the advisor creates the impression with the client (and with himself or herself) that the results are more than merely subjective and intuitive. Worse yet, the advisor may stop at this point feeling that he or she has completed the due diligence responsibility to "know the client." Here are some of the types of questionnaires that are out there.

SUBJECTIVE QUESTIONNAIRES

Psychological Profile
There are dozens of psychological profiles out there, and they consist of a series of questions that attempt to impute or predict investor behavior from the answers to the questions. I must admit that it is interesting to contemplate why investors behave in a certain manner. I have not seen a credible study showing a linkage between psychological profiles and a successful portfolio.

Statistical Questionnaire
I use a statistical questionnaire with clients. It is only a subjective tool for use in due diligence investigation. It has two

primary benefits: (1) It educates the client. The advisor can observe the client's reaction to the questions and suggest to him or her a different viewpoint when appropriate. A statistical questionnaire can also provide reinforcement about investment principles. (2) It serves as a catalyst to get the client thinking and talking about his or her feelings about investing. Clients rarely if ever have thought in depth about this topic, so this type of questionnaire helps bring to the surface any differences in views between partners.

Objective Method
I also use an *objective method* to quantify risk tolerance. This method will become clear as we work our way to the end of this chapter and into the next.

INVESTMENT GOALS

Here we document specific numeric targets for the portfolio. For a private client, the term we use is *target rate of return,* which means the return that the client needs from his or her investment assets to achieve his or her stated goals. How do I determine this return? I develop a comprehensive financial plan for each client.

The first step includes defining, with the client, his or her goals. Here are some examples of *quantifiable* goals:

1. Financial independence with a specified living standard
2. College funding for children or grandchildren
3. Purchase of real estate
4. Purchase of luxury cars
5. Seed money for a business venture
6. Purchase of a yacht

7. Gifts to family members and to charity

8. An emergency reserve

9. Minimum estate for heirs.

The word *quantifiable* is critical. There is no room here for loose, vague, or meaningless jargon. The goal must be specific and free of ambiguity. Furthermore, it must be easily translated into dollar cost terms as either a one-time cost or an expense stream or both. There must be a start date and an end date for each goal. Most important, it must be stated in terms that the client understands and agrees with. The second step is to prioritize and quantify these goals in today's dollars.

In some cases, I come to an agreement with the client in one sitting. In others, the client needs time to think through his or her priorities.

Third, in the client financial planning model, I enter each goal in dollar terms, and I give each one a start and completion date as desired by the client. This model takes into account all the details about client income, expenses, assets, and liabilities. I make assumptions about inflation of expenses and goals over time, and I assume a before-tax target rate of return for client investment assets. The model also calculates an income tax return each year for federal, state, and local taxes. These tax liabilities become part of cash flow. The plan is in balance when there is positive cash flow for each year in the plan over the projected lifetime of the client. The model also takes into account the requirement to pay estate and gift taxes. The client would not be around to worry about this—it falls on the shoulders of the heirs and the executors. Clients that I work with typically want to minimize the tax burden on their heirs. This can be another goal for the plan.

I rarely have a balanced plan on the first pass. In most cases, the cash requirements from income and investments exceed the goals in the plan. I then must work with the client to make the needed adjustments to the assumptions to bring the plan into balance. This may not require the elimination of a goal; rather, it may simply mean that I move the start of the goal to a later date. It may mean that the client must work for an additional year or two.

Next, I take note of the target rate of return used in the balanced plan. This return becomes our design point for our portfolio design model. I use our software to find the weighting of assets needed to reach this target rate of return with the least amount of risk.

This is our objective method for assessing risk tolerance and investment suitability. I take a pragmatic position about risk. I believe that the ultimate risk to clients is to have insufficient cash flow when they need it to fund their goals. All other definitions of *risk* are in a distant second place taken in this context. In most cases, this assessment covers the complete life cycle of the client. In some cases, it includes multiple generations.

> I believe that the ultimate risk to clients is to have insufficient cash flow when they need it to fund their goals.

This approach provides clients with an objective framework for deciding about risk. They can look at the portfolio design required to achieve the planned target rate of return, and if they feel uncomfortable about the portfolio design, they can alter the goals' framework. They can move a goal or two out in time, thus lowering the required target rate of return. This in turn means an investment mix that tilts to the conservative side of the spectrum.

INVESTMENT GUIDELINES

In this section, I document our policy about proxy voting, trading guidelines, and other operational considerations. Our focus here is to keep costs at a minimum. I also list here any required asset mix guidelines.

Asset mix guidelines can include restrictions placed by the client or client circumstances on securities or investment categories. It can cover assets already in the portfolio at the start of the advisor involvement. It might make sense, for example, to retain 5-year certificates of deposits (CDs) bought at a time when interest rates were high. There might be a restriction established by a trust to retain certain securities. The client may be uncomfortable with certain security types.

This is also the place to document restrictions suggested by the advisor. For example, an unrestricted asset allocation model may assign all financial assets to two or three categories or asset classes. Assume that such a portfolio is one of a family that represents the combination of assets that produces the specified return with the least amount of risk. Such a portfolio is theoretically sound. Still, you may feel that a strategy that calls for only two or three asset classes is too narrow in terms of diversification. Instead, you may wish to limit the maximum weighting to any investment category to, say, 20 or 25 percent of the total.

INVESTMENT PERFORMANCE REVIEW AND EVALUATION

This is the appropriate place for the documentation of reporting frequency and standards. The standards suggested by the Association for Investment Management Research (AIMR) and the Investment Management Consultants Association (IMCA) have more similarities

than differences. Both organizations have pamphlets available that describe these guidelines.

UPDATING THE IPS

The client should not view the IPS as something carved in
stone for the next millenium. Experience shows that
assumptions and circumstances change. That is why it
makes sense to periodically review the document for rele-
vance, which I do every year with each client. Here are
some additional benefits from the IPS update process:

- Provides a disciplined way for client to rethink
  priorities
- Incorporates recent historical data on each asset
  class
- Reflects changing assumptions about external
  forces
- Mirrors altered client circumstances
- Excludes goals already attained or no longer
  relevant

The Investment Policy Statement has a detailed 5-year,
front-end projection. Each year that I update the plan, I
move the 5-year plan forward by 1 year. The IPS becomes
the basis of communication and a reference point between
the client and the advisor. Each person knows what to
expect. My experience is that, with an IPS, clients have a
heightened level of comfort about the *how* and the *why* of
their asset deployment.

CHAPTER 3

Asset Class Portfolio Design

INTRODUCTION

In this chapter, I expect to lay the theoretical foundation for the rest of the book. I cannot emphasize enough the importance of this information for you the advisor. An Investment Policy Statement should contain the design of a portfolio for the client. That portfolio should have customization for that client. As an advisor and possibly a fiduciary, you have the responsibility to understand the theory behind any mathematical techniques that you use in the design process.

I plan to address this topic through a discussion of the contributions by the framers or founding fathers of portfolio theory. Many people have made valuable contributions to this topic, but here I will limit the discussion to four of the living legends of portfolio theory who, in my opinion, are the best of the best. This discussion touches only the highlights of the history of the development of Modern Portfolio Theory. I encourage you to go to your library and read the articles referenced here. That is your opportunity to peer over the shoulders of geniuses at work.

This book is not the forum to cover mathematical proofs. Instead, I have tried to capture in this chapter the essence of what the founding fathers concluded from their work. The emphasis is more on the contribution itself rather than on the line-by-line mathematical detail. I should say in passing that this approach does not let you or me off the hook. We need to understand the math as well. If it has been a while since you studied advanced mathematics, there may be a few cobwebs covering your quiver of advanced mathematical arrows. You need to brush those cobwebs away and get to the detail. If you expect to earn a professional designation such as Certified Financial Analyst (CFA) or Certified Investment Management Analyst (CIMA), you will have to know the math as well as the concepts.

MISTAKEN IDENTITY

I discern a feeling in some advisor circles that the theories to be discussed in this chapter are great for academic debate but are not for the real world. Au contraire! Harry Markowitz, Stephen Ross, and Barr Rosenberg all manage money applying the theories they each developed. All three manage money privately. For example, Ross serves as cochairman of Roll and Ross Asset Management Corp. with roughly $3 billion under management. Ross also is the Sterling Professor of Economics and Finance at Yale University. In addition, Markowitz offers a closed-end mutual fund, and Rosenberg offers an advisor-only, open-end mutual fund. Bill Sharpe is the only academic in the group. Even he has an extensive consulting practice working with investment committees of large pension and endowment funds.

THE THEORIES OF
HARRY M. MARKOWITZ

Harry Markowitz was born in Chicago. He attended the University of Chicago for his bachelor's, master's, and doctoral degrees. As a graduate student, he received an invitation to join the prestigious Cowles Commission for Research in Economics. This group produced a number of Nobel laureates.

In the early 1950s, Markowitz was a 24-year-old Ph.D. candidate. He needed a topic for his dissertation. A chance conversation produced a suggestion for a paper about the application of mathematical methods to the stock market. Markowitz describes what happened next in his autobiography:

> The basic concepts of portfolio theory came to me one afternoon in the library while reading John Burr Williams's Theory of Investment Value. Williams proposed that the value of a stock should equal the present value of its future dividends. Since future dividends are uncertain, I interpreted Williams's proposal to be to value a stock by its expected future dividends. But if the investor were only interested in expected values of securities, he or she would only be interested in the expected value of the portfolio; and to maximize the expected value of a portfolio one need invest only in a single security. This, I knew, was not the way investors did or should act. Investors diversify because they are concerned with risk as well as return. Variance came to mind as a measure of risk. The fact that portfolio variance depended on security covariances added to the plausibility of the approach. Since there were two criteria, risk and return, it was natural to assume that investors selected from the set of Pareto optimal risk-return combinations.[1]

----

1. Harry M. Markowitz, *Autobiography*, Appended to the Internet Web site for Nobel laureates: http://www.nobel.se/laureates/economy-1990-1-autobio.html.

In the course of writing this book, I have had the privilege of getting to know Harry Markowitz. In addition to being brilliant, I found him to be a gentleman and a very sincere human being. Dr. Markowitz gave me permission to share with you an interesting anecdote associated with his dissertation topic. Like many of us, he did not have a lot of extra spending money while in college. Consequently, he had little or no experience with investments and investing. To young Harry Markowitz, this project was merely an "intellectual exercise." Markowitz published his research in a 1952 paper[2] and a 1959 monograph.[3] Charles D. Ellis, a well-known contemporary investment strategist and money manager, prepared an anthology of investment classics, in which he made the following remark about Markowitz's 1952 paper:

> In this article, Harry Markowitz fired the shot heard "round the world," starting the intellectual campaign that led to modern portfolio theory and brought technology to investing.[4]

Markowitz won the Nobel Prize for economic science in 1990 for this pioneering work. The phrase used on the Nobel Web site to describe his contribution is "For having developed the theory of portfolio choice." Think about it for a minute: Something that started out to be an intellectual exercise ended up changing the course of history!

Something that started out to be an intellectual exercise ended up changing the course of history!

---

2. Harry M. Markowitz, "Portfolio Selection," *The Journal of Finance*, vol. 7, no. 1, March 1952, pp. 77–91 (New York: American Finance Association).

3. Harry M. Markowitz, *Portfolio Selection* (Blackwell, 1959).

4. Charles D. Ellis and James R. Vertin, *Classics—An Investor's Anthology* (Business One Irwin, The Institute of Chartered Financial Analysts, 1989), p. 277.

Now let us consider what Markowitz had to say. Remember that the idea of diversification was, at that time, an intuitive concept. It was not part of financial theory. Markowitz developed the formal theory of diversification. Perhaps the most profound insight of his work is that investments are risky when viewed in isolation. However, if an investment has a low correlation compared with other assets in the portfolio, it can actually reduce the overall risk of the portfolio.

> Perhaps the most profound insight of Markowitz's work is that investments are risky when viewed in isolation. However, if an investment has a low correlation compared with other assets in the portfolio, it can actually reduce the overall risk of the portfolio.

UNCERTAINTY

Investing and investments have certain common characteristics. The first is that all investment is in an environment of uncertainty. There are simply too many unknowns to forecast the future with certainty.

CORRELATION

Another common feature is the correlation among security returns. Returns on securities tend to move up and down together. Although securities are highly correlated, they are not perfectly correlated. For example, securities in the same industry are likely to have a higher correlation than securities in different industries. This principle implies that diversification can reduce risk but not eliminate it.

INVESTOR OBJECTIVES

Investors prefer high return to low return and certainty to uncertainty. After elimination of all portfolios that are inferior, there is remaining a set of portfolios referred to as "efficient." The choice among efficient portfolios depends on the degree of risk assumed by the investor.

MEASUREMENT OF UNCERTAINTY

One can also refer to uncertainty as "risk." Markowitz proposed the use of the statistical measurements of mean and variance to measure risk. The use of mean and variance as criteria is simplified if probability distributions are normal, that is, distributed in a bell-shaped fashion.[5]

Several important features of a normal distribution make the use of mean and variance as criteria at once simple and elegant: (1) It is *symmetric about the mean*—that is, half of the returns are below the mean, and half are above. (2) Because of this symmetry, the *mode* (most common) and the *median* (midpoint) are the same as the mean. (3) The area under the curve within 1 standard deviation of either side of the mean embraces roughly 68 percent of the total area under the curve. For 2 standard deviations, it includes 95 percent of the area. For 3 standard deviations, it covers 99.7 percent of the area. Knowing these characteristics, we can estimate the probabilities of exposure to returns that are 1, 2, and 3 standard deviations away from the mean.

Variance and its square root, the standard deviation, are the most common measures of variability or dispersion.

---

5. We will see later that this is a requirement only if we need to calculate the tails in the distribution.

Covariance and correlation define the relationship between random variables. They measure if and how there is a relationship. The diversification effect is at its best when you combine securities or assets with low correlation.

There is concern voiced among the critics of Mean-Variance Optimization (MVO) about the viability of the assumption of a normal distribution. Here is what Markowitz said, in a letter to me, on that question:

The story about mean-variance analysis and normal (Gaussian) distributions has at least three parts. Central to mean-variance analysis are two formulas:

$$E = X_1 m_1 + X_2 m_2 + \ldots + X_n m \tag{1}$$

$$V = X_1^2 V_1 + X_2^2 V_2 + \ldots V_n^2 V_n \tag{2}$$

$$+ 2(X_1 X_2 \sigma_{12} + X_1 X_3 \sigma_{13})$$

$$\ldots + X_{n-1} X_n \sigma_{13}$$

where E = The expected return of the portfolio
V = The variance of return of the portfolio
m_i = The mean (i.e., expected) return of the ith security
V_i = The variance of return of the ith security
σ_{ij} = The covariance of return between the ith and the jth security
X_i = The fraction of the portfolio invested in the ith security

Formula (1) relates the expected return of the portfolio to those securities and to amounts invested. Formula (2) relates the variance of the portfolio to the variances and covariances of securities as well as amounts invested.

Now, concerning Gaussian distributions: equations (1) and (2) do *not* depend on any assumption about normal distributions. They are always true (provided only that securities have finite means and variances; let's ignore the fact that some especially fat-tailed distributions can lack finite means or variances). So (ignoring the parenthetical caveat) it is always true that (1) and (2) may be used to compute estimated portfolio E and V from estimated securities' m_i V_i and σ_{ij}.

A. Next, suppose we know a portfolio's E and V, perhaps as computed by (1) and (2). Then we also know its standard deviation σ, since:

$$\sigma = \sqrt{V}$$

Now, may we say that there is a probability of 2.5 percent that return will be less than $E - 1.96\ \sigma$? Not unless we are willing to assume a Gaussian distribution. This is where the normal assumption comes in. We can use equations (1) and (2) to derive E, V, and σ; but we *cannot* use the normal table to calculate tails unless we make the normal assumption.

B. This leaves the following question. If distributions are not normal, is an investor well advised to use mean-variance analysis? Tobin [1958] says that mean-variance analysis assumes either a normal distribution or a quadratic utility function. This is not the Markowitz [1959] justification for mean-variance analysis. See the sections on pages 121 and 286–297. Better still, see the paper by Levy and Markowitz, "Approximating Expected Utility by a Function of Mean and Variance" [1979], *The American Economic Review*, vol. 69, no. 3, pp. 308–317.

The conclusion of the above is that, for a wide variety of utility functions and for probability distributions on portfolios, a carefully chosen mean-variance efficient portfolio can provide almost maximum utility.

In Levy-Markowitz note especially the distinction made between having a quadratic function versus one or another quadratic approximation to a given utility function. (The issue of whether mean-semi variance would give an even better approximation is not addressed in Levy-Markowitz and, to my knowledge, is still an open question.)

EXPECTED UTILITY MAXIM

Another concept that shaped his thinking was what he referred to as the "Expected Utility Maxim." He assumes that investors behave in a rational manner. They make decisions about their portfolios in the face of uncertainty. For each investor there is a set of characteristics that describe the preferences for that investor under conditions of uncertainty. For example, the curve for the preferences of an investor might look like that shown in Figure 3–1.

FIGURE 3-1

Expected Utility Maxim: Rational Investor
Markowitz (1952, 1959)

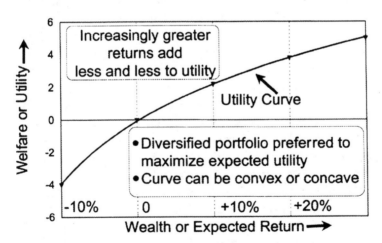

Source: Harry M. Markowitz, "Portfolio Selection," *The Journal of Finance*, vol. 7, no. 1, March 1952, pp. 77–91 (New York: American Finance Association), and *Portfolio Selection* (Blackwell, 1959).

Values on the horizontal axis represent wealth or expected return. Values on the vertical axis represent benefit, welfare, or utility. For the hypothetical investor illustrated in Figure 3–1, increasingly greater returns add less and less utility. Some people refer to this feature as *diminishing marginal utility*. Note that the shape of the utility curve for this investor is *concave* (open portion is down). Another investor might have a utility curve that is *convex* in shape (open portion is up). A third investor might have a utility curve that is *both concave and convex*.

There is another way to think about Figure 3–1—that is, as describing the degree to which the individual will take risks for outcomes presented along the horizontal axis. Investors prefer a diversified portfolio in order to maximize expected utility.

PORTFOLIO OPTIMIZATION

Next, consider Figure 3–2. This is a view at the portfolio level. Plotted on the vertical axis is the expected return. On the horizontal axis is risk as measured by the standard deviation. Each point on the curve AB represents a portfolio with a mixture of securities. Any point on the AB curve is what Markowitz refers to as an "efficient" set. The curve AB is an "efficient frontier." Markowitz also referred to the technique as "Mean Variance Optimization," or MVO.

Consider these examples. Assume that we have the portfolio represented by the point X on Figure 3–2. This portfolio is not as efficient or productive as those on curve AB. Portfolio Y provides *more return* than X at the *same risk* as X. Portfolio Z provides the *same return* as X but with *less risk* than X. You can say that portfolios Y and Z provide greater utility than does portfolio X.

With a normal distribution, the investor needs only the

FIGURE 3–2

MPT Efficient Frontier
Markowitz (1952)

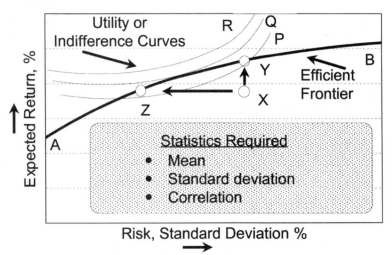

Source: Harry M. Markowitz, "Portfolio Selection," *The Journal of Finance,* vol. 7, no. 1, March 1952, pp. 77–91 (New York: American Finance Association).

(1) mean, (2) the standard deviation, and (3) the correlation for each security with other securities to define a portfolio. Think about that: There is no fundamental data such as price-earnings ratio or dividend yield mentioned here! This was radical stuff for the time!

Next, look at the curves labeled *P, Q,* and *R* at the top of Figure 3–2. These are utility or indifference curves. Each investor has a unique grouping of parallel or nested utility curves. Some people refer to them as *iso-utility curves.* Tracing a curve through all the combinations of expected return and risk with equal expected utility creates *one* of the utility curves within the nested set. Consider these analogies. You can think of these as lines of constant temperature on a weather map or constant altitude on a topological map.

The mathematical function that represents these iso-utility curves must reflect the option to demand more return for taking more risk. The point of tangency between a utility curve, Q in this case, and the efficient frontier represents the precise combination of expected return and risk that maximizes the expected utility for this specific investor. It matches investor preference for incurring risk in order to increase expected return. It also provides the best available tradeoff of risk and return. It is the highest and best use of the securities under consideration. It is the most efficient, the most productive portfolio for this investor.

SINGLE-FACTOR MODEL

Markowitz realized that his theories required an enormous amount of computing power. He offered several examples in his 1959 book to illustrate this. Suppose we have a portfolio of 500 securities. We want to compute the efficient frontier for this portfolio. This requires the computation of 500 expected returns, 500 variances, and 124,750 covariances. For computers of today, this is quite manageable. In the early 1950s, we were just breaking out of the punched card machine era. Computers were not in widespread use at that time.

This problem prompted Markowitz [1959] to propose a *single-factor model*. Figure 3–3 illustrates his proposal: On the vertical axis is the return of a security; on the horizontal axis is the return of an index. He suggested that you could explain the correlation between two securities in terms of their correlation with an index. The equation at the top of the figure appears in his 1959 book. We compute a regres-

FIGURE 3-3

Single-Factor Model
Markowitz (1959)

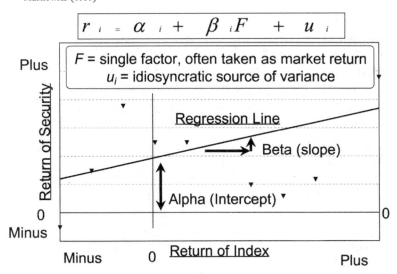

$$r_i = \alpha_i + \beta_i F + u_i$$

F = single factor, often taken as market return
u_i = idiosyncratic source of variance

Plus

Return of Security

Regression Line

Beta (slope)

Alpha (Intercept)

0

Minus

Minus   0   Return of Index   Plus

Source: Harry M. Markowitz, *Portfolio Selection* (Blackwell, 1959).

sion (least-squares) line through the data. This is a straight line of the form $y = (m)(x) + b$ that we all learned in secondary school. The slope of the line is the *beta* of the security. The intercept with the zero vertical axis is a term called *alpha*.

You can engage Dr. Markowitz as a portfolio manager. The Japan Equity Fund [symbol JEQ, traded on the New York Stock Exchange (NYSE) as a closed-end fund] has him as the portfolio manager. You may find comfort in knowing that Dr. Markowitz and his team make use of Modern Portfolio Theory to manage the fund.

THE THEORIES OF
WILLIAM F. SHARPE

After completing his graduate work at the University of Chicago, Markowitz moved to California. There he joined the Rand Corporation. It was while he was at Rand that he met Bill Sharpe. William F. Sharpe shared the Nobel Prize in 1990 with Harry Markowitz and Merton Miller. Sharpe received recognition for his work on the *Capital Asset Pricing Model* (CAPM). The wording on the Nobel Web site for Sharpe's award is "For his contributions to the theory of price formation for financial assets, the so-called Capital Asset Pricing Model (CAPM)."

Sharpe contacted Markowitz at Rand. Sharpe wanted Markowitz to act as advisor for his Ph.D. dissertation. Markowitz suggested an application of the one-factor model proposed in Markowitz [1959]. Sharpe published the results of that work in 1963.[6] It is a market model using what is known as *normative theory.* It is a one-factor model of covariance (see Figure 3–4). It made assumptions consistent with Markowitz's MVO theory:

1. MVO is not required for all investors.
2. All investors need not hold the same beliefs.
3. The market as a whole need not be part of the efficient set.

---

6. William F. Sharpe, "A Simplified Model for Portfolio Analysis," *Management Science,* vol. 9, no. 2, 1963, pp. 277–293.

FIGURE 3-4

Market Model—Normative Theory: One-Factor Model
of Covariance
Sharpe (1963)

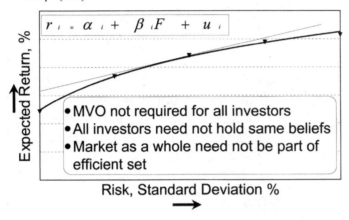

$$r_i = \alpha_i + \beta_i F + u_i$$

Expected Return, %

- MVO not required for all investors
- All investors need not hold same beliefs
- Market as a whole need not be part of efficient set

Risk, Standard Deviation %

Source: William F. Sharpe, "A Simplified Model for Portfolio Analysis," *Management Science*, vol. 9, no. 2, 1963, pp. 277–293.

CAPITAL ASSET PRICING MODEL

In 1964, Sharpe published his famous paper about CAPM.[7] I framed it graphically in Figure 3–5. On the surface, this picture looks much the same as Figure 3–4. In reality, it is quite different in its assumptions and results. It is also quite different than the Markowitz MVO illustrated in Figure 3–2. CAPM assumes that the market is in equilibrium. It

7. William F. Sharpe, "Capital Asset Prices: A Theory of Market Equilibrium Under Conditions of Risk," *The Journal of Finance,* vol. 19, no. 3, September 1964, pp. 425–442.

FIGURE 3–5

Capital Asset Pricing Model: Positive Theory
Sharpe (1964)

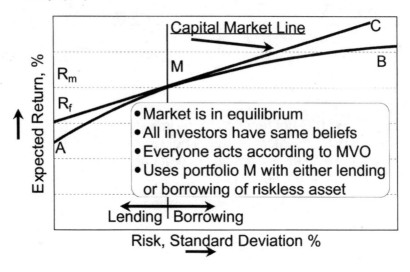

Source: William F. Sharpe, "Capital Asset Prices: A Theory of Market Equilibrium Under Conditions of Risk,"
The Journal of Finance, vol. 19, no. 3, September 1964, pp. 425–442.

says that all investors have the same beliefs and behave
alike concerning risk and expected return. It assumes that
everyone acts according to MVO. Markowitz's MVO makes
none of these assumptions.

There is another important assumption for CAPM.
Instead of individual securities, it assumes that the investor
has the choice of two investments. One is a market portfolio noted on Figure 3–5 as *M*. This is a basket of worldwide
securities all at a state of equilibrium. *M* is by definition an
efficient portfolio. The other investment available to the
investor in the CAPM world is a risk-free asset shown here

as R_f. The line drawn from R_f through the point of tangency at M up to C is the *capital market line*.

In the idealized CAPM world, investors adjust their portfolios up and down the capital market line. At point M they are 100 percent in the market portfolio. They can lower their risk profile by moving down the capital market line. They do this by placing part of the portfolio in the risk-free asset R_f. CAPM assumes that the mix of the remaining portion is the same as M, the market portfolio. The process of moving down the capital market line is called *lending*. Investors can also raise the risk level (and return) of their CAPM portfolio through *borrowing* the risk-free asset R_f and investing the borrowed amount in additional M. Today, CAPM is still a major analytical tool used for explaining phenomena observed in capital markets for risky assets.

Figure 3–6 illustrates an additional outgrowth of CAPM. On the vertical axis we have expected return. On the horizontal axis, we have risk expressed *not* as standard deviation but as beta. An assumption of CAPM is that you can subdivide the standard deviation into two components. One component can be neutralized through diversification; the other component cannot be diversified away. The beta within CAPM is a measure of the component of standard deviation of this nondiversifiable component.

In Figure 3–6, R_f is the risk-free asset, R_m is the risk of the market, beta$_i$ is the nondiversifiable risk of the security, and M is the market. The beta of M is 1. The beta of R_f is zero. Betas for securities riskier than the market have a beta greater than 1. The line R_f to C is known as the *security market line*. It is *not* the same as the capital market line from Figure 3–5. There is often confusion on this point, so take the time to think it through so that you understand the difference.

As I write this, Dr. Sharpe has an affiliation with

FIGURE 3–6

CAPM and Security Market Line: Individual Security Expected
Return and Beta
Sharpe (1964)

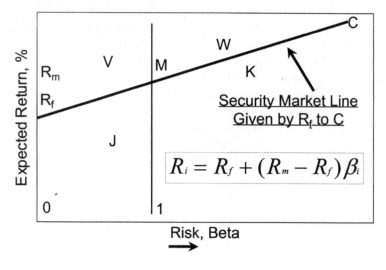

Source: William F. Sharpe, "Capital Asset Prices: A Theory of Market Equilibrium Under Conditions of
Risk," *The Journal of Finance,* vol. 19, no. 3, September 1964, pp. 425–442.

Stanford University in California. He is the author of many
books and papers on investing, and he serves on the investment committees of institutional investors. He has a helpful
Web site on the Internet.[8] Dr. Sharpe also did pioneering
work in the area of investment manager style analysis. I
plan to discuss that in another chapter.

---

8. http://gsb-www.stanford.edu/~wfsharpe/home.htm. If there is any cer-
    tainty in life, it is that Web addresses change over time. If this one does
    not work, look for "William Sharpe" using the search routines that came
    with your Web browser.

THE "TWO-BETA" TRAP

The mathematics and the nuances of MVO versus CAPM are not easy subjects to master. Many people make the mistake of merging the two together in their heads. A lot of us have been in that boat. Some of us still are and do not know it. The misunderstanding and confusion on this point came to a boil during the early 1980s. Harry Markowitz felt the need to set the record straight. He published an article in 1984[9] to outline the differences between the MVO Normative Model and the CAPM Positive Model. The Markowitz article does an excellent job of positioning the two theories.[10] I view it as required reading for you and me.

PRUDENT INVESTOR RULES

MPT is also imbedded in our legal system. The latest manifestation is the *Third Restatement of the Law of Trusts— Prudent Investor Rules.*[11] The American Law Institute in Washington, D.C., adopted and promulgated this document starting in 1990. I recommend that you read it. It appears to be the foundation for the law in most states. I expect every state to adopt it eventually. *Prudent Investor Rules* will be the basis for decisions by the courts concerning qualified retirement plans. This document also heavily influences court rulings about investments associated with

---

9. Harry M. Markowitz, "The 'Two Beta' Trap," *The Journal of Portfolio Management*, vol. 11, no. 1, Fall 1994, pp. 12–20.
10. I used software to produce efficient frontier examples for illustrations in this book. The primary calculation technique makes use of the MVO Normative Model. There are no calculations using CAPM. Please keep this in mind as you view the illustrations.
11. *Third Restatement of the Law of Trusts—Prudent Investor Rules* (St. Paul, Minn.: American Law Institute Publishers, 1992).

trusts. In my opinion, *Prudent Investor Rules* should be the standard applied by the advisor to portfolio design for private clients. For a practitioner discussion of *Prudent Investor Rules* and ERISA compliance, see *The Management of Investment Decisions.*[12]

THE THEORIES OF STEPHEN A. ROSS

The next major milestone in the evolution of portfolio theory came with a paper from Stephen A. Ross.[13] There he introduced Arbitrage Pricing Theory, or APT. APT is an attempt to loosen the rigidity found in the assumptions of CAPM. Ross wanted APT to be closer to reality. Here some of the assumptions he used:

1. There are many sources of risk and uncertainty.
2. There is no longer an assumption of a single-factor model with a single portfolio for all investors. Ross replaces this with a multifactor model that drives asset returns. The factors are macroeconomic in nature. According to Ross the factors that explain security returns reasonably well are (a) surprises in inflation, (b) surprises in the economy (gross national product, or GNP), (c) surprises in investor confidence (measured by the corporate bond premium), and (d) shifts in the yield curve. Ross assumes that you cannot avoid these factors, but you can steer your portfolio away from them.

---

12. Donald B. Trone, William R. Allbright, and Philip R. Taylor, *The Management of Investment Decisions* (Chicago: Irwin Professional Publishing, 1996).
13. Stephen A. Ross, "The Arbitrage Theory of Capital Asset Pricing," *Journal of Economic Theory,* vol. 13, 1976, pp. 341–360.

3. APT suggests that investors will price these factors accurately. They are sources of risk that cannot be diversified away. Investors demand compensation in the form of expected return for holding securities exposed to these risks. APT also uses the term *beta* to measure this risk exposure.

4. Investors choose their portfolio with a customized array of betas based on their unique risk preferences.

5. Mispricing occurs in the investment world. Investors attempt to identify these price discontinuities and exploit them through arbitrage as they find them.

You can see from this that there is considerable difference between APT and CAPM. You may wish to think of it this way. If CAPM is a specialty store that offers one-size-fits-all clothing, APT is a haberdashery that offers tailored suits and dresses.

Remember that CAPM assumes that all investors:

a. Seek mean-variance efficiency

b. Have the same beliefs

c. Can lend all they have or borrow all they want at the riskless rate

Here is what Markowitz [1991 notes to 1959 book] says about APT given these CAPM assumptions:

> The arbitrage pricing theory (APT) of Ross [1976] drops (the) assumption (a) that investors seek mean-variance efficiency, retains (b) and (c) and assumes a multifactor model of covariance discussed in the note on Chapter IV. Its conclusions are somewhat like those of traditional CAPMs [i.e., those with assumptions (a) − (c) or (a) − (c')], as compared with the CAPM of Markowitz 1987, in that the APT

premises imply that the market portfolio is an efficient portfolio in the sense that it could be held by a rational investor,
and expected returns are linearly related to the Beta$_{iK}$ of
equation (7) in the note on Chapter IV.

There is a firm with an APT offering that you can try:
MacWorld. With it you can get a feel for how APT works.
You can find information about MacWorld at their Web
site.[14] They use APT to forecast returns for markets, stocks,
and mutual funds.

Why has APT not been widely used by institutional
investors to replace CAPM? Here is one possible explanation for this puzzle.[15] (In the interests of full disclosure, one
of the authors of this explanation is Dr. William Sharpe, the
framer of CAPM.):

> Despite its attractive features, APT has not been widely
> applied by the investment community. The reason lies
> largely with APT's most significant drawback: the lack of
> specificity regarding the multiple factors that systematically
> affect security returns as well as the long-term return asso-
> ciated with each of the factors. Rightly or wrongly, CAPM
> unambiguously states that a security's covariance with the
> market portfolio is the only systematic risk within a well-
> diversified portfolio. APT, conversely, is conspicuously
> silent regarding the particular systematic factors affecting a
> security's risk and return. Investors must fend for them-
> selves in determining these factors.

14. MacWorld, http://www.mworld.com/. This is the Web site for MacWorld.
15. William F. Sharpe, Gordon Alexander, and Jeffrey V. Bailey, *Investments*
   (Englewood Cliffs, N.J.: Prentice-Hall, 1995), p. 333.

THE THEORIES OF BARR ROSENBERG

Barr Rosenberg introduced another model of covariance.[16] It is a multifactor model including not only macroeconomic factors but also *industry* factors. It is widely used today.

Rosenberg formed a company known as BARRA. While Rosenberg himself is no longer there, you can find the descendents of his multifactor models at BARRA. You can find a discussion of the models on their Web site on the Internet.[17] They currently have up to 12 factors in their Single Country Equity Risk Models. The number of factors they include depends on the subject country. They currently have models representing 13 foreign countries. They have four variations of an equity model for the United States. Here are the 12 factors they use at the moment: volatility, momentum, size, liquidity, growth, value, earnings variation, financial leverage, foreign sensitivity, labor intensity, yield, and low capitalization.

ASSET CLASS INVESTING

WHAT IS IT?

Let us define an *asset class* as a grouping of investments with similar return and risk characteristics. There is similarity in behavior. The common investments tend to move in harmony or sympathy with each other. Statisticians say

---

16. Barr Rosenberg, "Extra-Market Components of Covariance in Security Returns," *Journal of Financial and Quantitative Analysis,* March 1974, pp. 263–274.
17. BARRA, http://www.barra.com/index.html. This is the Web site for BARRA. If this address does not work, try the search routines on your Web browser.

that there is a high degree of correlation between the investments within the class. To paraphrase an old saying from
Washington, investments that look, quack, and waddle in
the same way are most likely in the *same asset class*.

WHAT ARE EXAMPLES OF ASSET CLASSES?

Portfolio design is as much art as science, and no two advisors use the same set of asset classes. There is a law of
motion, however, as applied to investments. It says that all
free markets move in cycles. To take advantage of that law,
the advisor can suggest a variety of asset classes that move
in dissimilar cycles. For better or worse, here is my list:

Large stocks
Small stocks
International stocks
Emerging countries
Intermediate-term bonds
High-yield bonds
Real estate
Natural resources
Short-term bonds
Cash equivalents

Figure 3–7 shows each asset class on a graph of return versus risk. In this case, return is total return, and risk is the
standard deviation of those returns. *Standard deviation* is the
variation of the return about the mean or average return.
You can see the positioning of each asset versus the others.

In the implementation of our portfolio design, we typically use a mixture of core, growth, and value mutual
funds in the large and small stock asset classes. Bond funds

Scenario Assumptions Graph

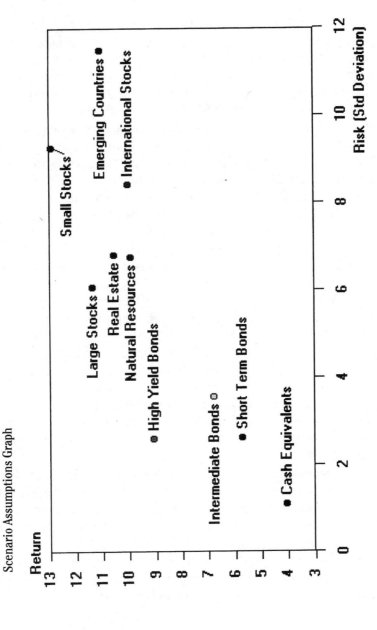

Software: Frontier Analytics, Inc., Investment Plus.

provide added stability to the portfolio. High-yield bond funds approach stocklike returns with about half the risk of stocks. Notice the real estate and natural resources. For some clients we use direct investments or private placements for these classes. Private placements often require a minimum investment of $100,000. For other clients we use mutual funds. The returns shown here are for index proxies that are financial assets with investments in these classes. On a few occasions, our clients act as "angels" and make venture capital investments. When they do, we add venture capital as an asset class. To implement this class in mutual fund format, you may wish to consider the growing number of micro-cap stock mutual funds.

Figure 3–8 shows the results of the correlation calculation between each pair of asset classes that we normally use. A value of +1.00 in the body of the table reflects a perfect correlation. A value of zero reflects no correlation. A value of −1.00 reflects perfect negative correlation. International stocks, for example, have a +0.43 correlation with large stocks. *High-yield bonds* have a +0.48 correlation with large stocks. Figures 3–9 and 3–10 show a history of the correlation for international stocks and for high-yield bonds with large stocks. *Low correlation* means that the asset has a better chance of having peaks and valleys at times that are different from that of the other asset in the pair under consideration.

The assumption here is that the portfolio is a qualified retirement plan, or an *individual retirement account* (IRA). Current taxation is not an issue. If a client has one or more taxable accounts, I do a portfolio design for these on an after-tax basis. There I take into account the tax bracket of the client, the capital gains rate, and the tax rates for state and local governments. I consider the turnover rate of each asset class, along with the transaction costs of each class. I

Scenario Correlation Table

Asset Class	[1]	[2]	[3]	[4]	[5]	[6]	[7]	[8]	[9]	[10]
[1] Large Stocks	1.00	0.76	0.43	0.36	0.32	0.48	0.55	0.60	0.26	-0.06
[2] Small Stocks	0.76	1.00	0.35	0.32	0.15	0.37	0.46	0.53	0.10	-0.05
[3] International Stocks	0.43	0.35	1.00	0.16	0.22	0.26	0.27	0.27	0.19	-0.10
[4] Emerging Countries	0.36	0.32	0.16	1.00	0.06	0.17	0.22	0.26	0.03	0.01
[5] Intermediate Bonds	0.32	0.15	0.22	0.06	1.00	0.45	0.20	0.05	0.90	-0.01
[6] High Yield Bonds	0.48	0.37	0.26	0.17	0.45	1.00	0.30	0.26	0.42	-0.07
[7] Real Estate	0.55	0.46	0.27	0.22	0.20	0.30	1.00	0.36	0.15	-0.10
[8] Natural Resources	0.60	0.53	0.27	0.26	0.05	0.26	0.36	1.00	0.01	0.05
[9] Short Term Bonds	0.26	0.10	0.19	0.03	0.90	0.42	0.15	0.01	1.00	0.04
[10] Cash Equivalents	-0.06	-0.05	-0.10	0.01	-0.01	-0.07	-0.10	0.05	0.04	1.00

Software: Frontier Analytics, Inc., Investment Plus.

FIGURE 3-9

Correlation Graph: Large Stocks versus International Stocks
Rolling 1-Year Periods

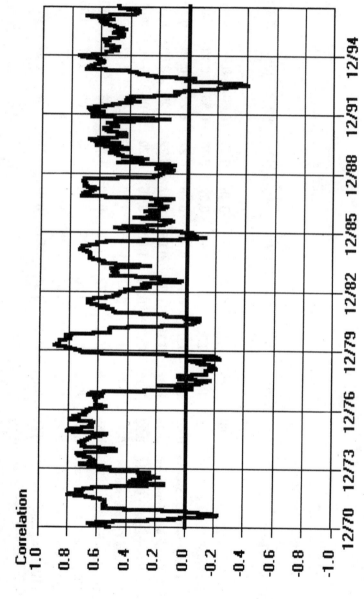

Software: Frontier Analytics, Inc., Investment Plus.

Correlation Graph: Large Stocks versus High-Yield Bonds
Rolling 1-Year Periods

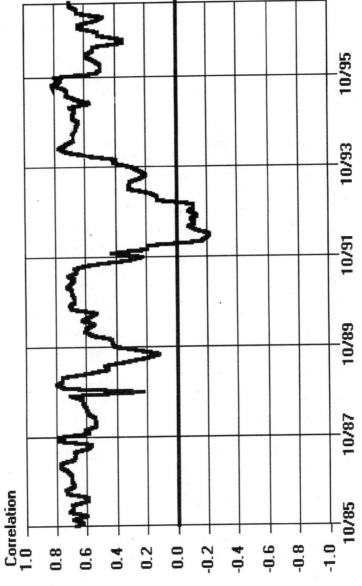

Software: Frontier Analytics, Inc., Investment Plus.

suggest that you do a side-by-side design of a nontaxable versus a taxable hypothetical portfolio. Keep all other assumptions the same for the two accounts. Assume that the client is in the highest tax bracket. Look at the resulting asset allocations along each frontier for an equivalent return. You will see that they are not the same. Taxable clients appreciate attention to this subtlety by their advisors.

Most of my clients prefer that I *not* have a substantial weighting in cash equivalents in their portfolio. Why then is cash equivalents an asset class here? Cash has good news and bad news elements. I use it first as an educational tool. I show them that holding some cash can be an excellent way to lower the risk profile and provide added stability to a portfolio as a whole. Second, there are cases in which clients need immediate liquidity. They want the ability to ask for a wire transfer or write a check on the day they need the money. Having cash as an asset class allows me to show them the impact on their overall portfolio. Third, some clients may be going through a turbulent period in their lives. Their job or business may have adverse exposures. They may need a certain amount of cash there for comfort so they can sleep at night.

The client may express a strong preference to stay "fully invested." I then exclude cash equivalents as an asset class. Notice that I still have short-term bond funds to act as a reasonable surrogate for cash equivalents. The model excludes this class for portfolios on the aggressive end of the spectrum. Our clients have far less objection to this asset class than to cash.

There is another point to consider about the need for cash equivalents. Most mutual fund supermarket brokers have an account category that allows both margin and check writing. The client often finds it difficult to forecast cash flow needs. Without the needed cash equivalents, I suggest that the client transact a wire transfer or write a check. With accounts that are fully invested, either action creates a margin loan. Then we satisfy the loan and trim the portfolio by liquidating a portion of some asset class that is overextended in terms of targeted weightings.

THE CONTRIBUTIONS OF GARY BRINSON, RANDOLPH HOOD, BRIAN D. SINGER, AND GILBERT BEEBOWER

Gary Brinson, together with Randolph Hood, Brian D. Singer, and Gilbert Beebower, made a valuable contribution to the art and science of portfolio design. In 1986, they conducted an empirical study of 91 large pension funds.[18] They performed attribution analysis on the data. They wanted to know to what degree (1) investment policy, (2) market timing, and (3) security selection influenced actual portfolio returns. The results showed an overwhelming contribution by investment policy decisions. Investment committees historically spent most of their time on the selection of money managers. The 1986 study suggested that this was misplaced emphasis. The first study created some controversy. Five years later there was a repeat of the study.[19] This time the subject was 82 large pension funds. The results were roughly the same as the 1986 study. Figure 3–11 shows the

---

18. Gary P. Brinson, L. Randolph Hood, and Gilbert L. Beebower, "Determinants of Portfolio Performance," *Financial Analysts Journal*, July–August 1986, pp. 39–44.
19. Gary P. Brinson, Brian D. Singer, and Gilbert L. Beebower, "Determinants of Portfolio Performance II: An Update," *Financial Analysts Journal*, May–June 1991, pp. 40–48.

F I G U R E 3–11

Determinants of Portfolio Performance: Large U.S. Pension Plans

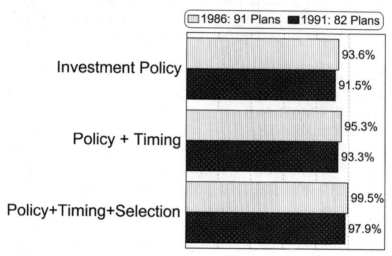

Source: Gary P. Brinson, L. Randolph Hood, and Gilbert L. Beebower, "Determinants of Portfolio Performance," *Financial Analysts Journal,* July–August 1986, pp. 39–44, and Gary P. Brinson, Brian D. Singer, and Gilbert L. Beebower, "Determinants of Portfolio Performance II: An Update," *Financial Analysts Journal,* May–June 1991, pp. 40–48.

results in graphical form. Over 90 percent of the investment return of these plans is from *policy decisions. Policy* as used here means the choice of *which asset classes* to be in and *how much to allocate* to those classes. These studies gave those advocating passive management strategies considerable ammunition for the ongoing passive-versus-active debate. I plan to discuss this subject in later chapters.

Before we accept these study results as dogma, I want to offer a small caveat. The subjects of the two studies were some of the largest pension funds in the country. These funds, because of their size, have practical limitations on the types of securities they can buy. You can think of it as the battleship *New Jersey* attempting to make a U turn in New York City's East River. The battleship needs *liquidity* (pun intended) to make the turn. The securities that these large pension funds buy must likewise have a certain minimum liquidity as determined by their market capitalization. The large funds also do not bear the burden of tax considerations.

Now consider the focus of this book—the Private Client. Let us continue with the naval metaphor. Financial assets of a typical private client are smaller by comparison. It is like a launch used to transport crew members to and from the battleship. A private client has the luxury of buying smaller capitalization securities if that is part of the strategy. However, these are, of course, less efficient asset classes. There are fewer analysts who follow small stocks than follow large stocks; furthermore, private clients must consider taxes for portfolio design.

To my knowledge, no studies equivalent to the two Brinson studies cited here exist for the private client market. We cannot say with theoretical rigor or even with empirical evidence that the Brinson et al., results apply to our private client portfolios. This is not to say that we should ignore the studies. We can, I believe, infer a strong relationship to the smaller portfolio. Let us say, hypothetically, that a similar study of private client portfolios showed only a 50 percent attribution to investment policy decisions. It would still be of major importance. For the Private Client, I have to rely in the end on common sense. It is my conclusion that time spent during portfolio design on investment policy decisions is time well spent.

THE CONTRIBUTIONS OF
EUGENE FAMA AND
KENNETH FRENCH

CAPM and the two pension fund studies cited above support the argument that markets are efficient. They helped to clarify positions on both sides of the mythical line-in-the-sand in the active-versus-passive debate.

In 1996, two highly respected academics, Eugene Fama and Kenneth French, broke ranks with the MPT mantra and reshaped the debate.[20] They published a study showing that there is an opportunity for active management after all. They found that strategies that concentrate on high-book-to-market stocks tend to have superior returns. Value styles including the high-book-to-market approach are part of the discussion of active management found in Chapter 4.

ASSET CLASS ASSUMPTIONS

I use asset allocation software to do the thousands of calculations needed to find results suitable for the client. Let us turn our attention to the process of deciding about appropriate input data for the model.

WHICH ASSET CLASSES?

We must choose which asset classes to use. Let us assume that they are those found in Figure 3–7. We then select a suitable index to act as a proxy for each asset class. An index

---

20. Eugene F. Fama and Kenneth R. French, "Multifactor Explanations of Asset Pricing Anomalies," *The Journal of Finance*, March 1996, pp. 55–84.

that spans multiple cycles is preferable. Figure 3–12 shows the index proxies assumed for this book. This is not to say that they are the only indices suitable for this task.

FORECASTING EXPECTED RETURNS

All asset allocation optimizers require a forecast for each asset class. That includes expected return, risk, and correlation. When you use the software, you take responsibility for the forecast—that is, the client views it as your forecast. This forecast becomes critical. The results have great sensitivity to this forecast. Look for example at expected returns shown in Figure 3–13. Let us say that our finest effort (or that of the analyst we use) produces a most likely return over the long term of 9 percent. Now say that we are off by only 1 percent in either direction. If we are too conservative by 1 percent, our terminal value is 20 percent higher than expected. If we are too optimistic by 1 percent, our terminal value is 17 percent lower than expected.

"As-Is" Method

All asset allocation software that I know about comes with default values for expected returns. Some software suppliers withhold details about their calculations of expected returns. If that is the case, look for another supplier because this information is crucial. Other suppliers have these return values "hard-wired" into the software—that is, you cannot change them. (Presumably, the vendor assumes that they know what is best and want to protect you from yourself.) I personally avoid these also. I prefer to have the option to modify the expected returns for any asset class. For those remaining vendors, several questions arise: How did the software supplier arrive at these values? Do you

Index Proxies for Asset Classes

Asset Class	Index Proxy
Large Stocks	Standard & Poor's 500 Stocks
Small Stocks	Dimensional Fund Advisors US 9/10 Small Co
International Stocks	Morgan Stanley Capital International EAFE® Index-$
Emerging Countries	Morgan Stanley Capital International Emerging Free Markets-$
Intermediate Bonds	Merrill Lynch Corporate 5-9.9 yrs
High Yield Bonds	Merrill Lynch High Yield Master
Real Estate	National Association of Real Estate Investment Trusts ® -Equity Index
Natural Resources	American Stock Exchange Oil
Short Term Bonds	Merrill Lynch Corporate 3-4.9 yrs
Cash Equivalents	Federal 3-mo Treasury bills

Source: Large stocks: Reprinted by permission of Standard & Poor's, a division of The McGraw-Hill Companies. Small stocks: Courtesy Dimensional Fund Advisors Inc. International stocks and emerging countries: Morgan Stanley Capital International. Intermediate bonds, high-yield bonds, and short-term bonds: Reprinted by permission of Merrill Lynch, Pierce, Fenner & Smith Incorporated. Copyright Merrill Lynch, Pierce, Fenner & Smith Incorporated. Real estate: NAREIT Index used with permission. Natural resources: Used with permission of the American Stock Exchange, Inc.

FIGURE 3–13

Sensitivity of Forecast to Data: Expected Return Is 9 Percent
Terminal Value on $1 Million in 20 Years

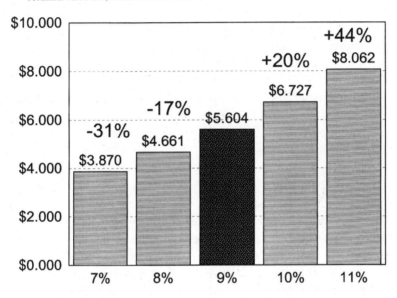

understand their method? Do you agree with their method? Here are some methods they may use to derive expected returns.

Analyst Estimates
Some suppliers of asset allocation software derive their forecasted returns from work by research analysts. The supplier may have these analysts on staff, or they may retain the services of an outside firm. At times I read or hear arguments from advisors in support of this method. The essence of the argument is that these forecasts are the work of a group of analysts with credentials and résumés as long as

your arm. They argue that these forecasts are the output from the best and the brightest.

I have a problem with this logic. I have nothing against any research analyst or firm. The problem comes from the lack of agreement between different firms that provide this information. Their analysts have equally impeccable credentials. The only thing consistent in the forecasts from firm to firm is the absence of consistency. Is my army of Ph.D.s better or worse than your army of Ph.D.s? I do not think so. Is there a service out there that keeps a scorecard about the accuracy of these forecasts? If so, please call my office immediately.

Long-Term Historical
Returns Method

This method is easy to understand. In my opinion, it should be your method of choice unless you have a substantiated reason to have confidence in another approach. Expected returns, standard deviations, and correlation coefficients are an arithmetic average of each year for the historical period. A key to this method is the phrase "long term." I like to use as much history as is available, preferably at least 30 years.

Some argue that the historical method is inappropriate because it is *what has happened* rather than *what will happen*. They seem to argue that their forecast is forward-looking and, therefore, must presumably be correct. This argument has an appealing sound and looks great on paper but rapidly withers under the heat of the sun lamp. It presumes that the supplier *knows what will happen!* Give me a break! Where is the track record, empirical studies, or even back testing to support this claim?

Building-Blocks Method

One advocate for this method is the Chicago-based Ibbotson Associates. You can find a synopsis of it in the *Journal of Financial Planning*.[21] I agree with the basic concept. This method seems simple on the surface, but it has some complex subtleties. The concept is that each asset class provides a reward to investors for taking additional risk beyond that of a risk-free asset. They refer to this reward as the "risk premium." The expected return is the total of this risk-premium plus the risk-free rate.

The risk-free component of the building-blocks method reflects current market expectations. The Ibbotson position is that the "risk-free" rate is the income component of a treasury that *matches the time horizon of the investor*. Thus, it could be the income return of a 1-year, 5-year, or 20-year treasury. Ibbotson suggests that zero-coupon bonds best represent this income component of treasuries. Their rationale is that it permits the marketplace to specify the horizon premium of treasuries with different terms. Their goal is to reflect "current market expectations as much as possible." For an investor with a 20-year time horizon, the risk-free rate is that of a 20-year zero.

The risk premium for large-cap stocks is the difference between the arithmetic mean of annual income returns on long-term treasuries and the arithmetic mean of annual total returns on large-cap stocks. The method uses a similar approach for other asset classes. Small stocks have a small-

---

21. Lori Lucas, "Building Better Optimization Inputs," *Journal of Financial Planning*, February 1996, pp. 64–67.

stock premium that is the excess return over large-stock premiums. Corporate bonds have a default premium.

The return expectation for equities in the Ibbotson article using the building-blocks method is 15.3 percent for large stocks and 17.7 percent for small stocks. As a practitioner, this is the place on the trail where I get uncomfortable. These returns are substantially above those of long-term history.[22]

You must decide if you are comfortable setting client expectations at these levels. My clients react much better to surprises on the upside rather than the downside. Of course, that is just my opinion. I could be wrong.

CAVEATS

I. Computer model design has come a long way. Designers today have sensitivity to making models user-friendly. Any person can push a few buttons and see the screen light up. Beware! One should not blindly accept the results of any computer-generated model. Use of these models with no understanding of the assumptions, the methods, the math, and the data is a recipe for disaster!

II. The results must also withstand the test of advisor

---

22. Part of this difference is due to the choice of averaging method. For multiple holding periods, an arithmetic average exceeds a geometric average except when holding-period returns are all the same. Generally, the geometric average is a better method to estimate the probability distribution of terminal wealth. That is what our clients have the most interest in knowing. For more information about estimating expected returns and future value, see Mark Kritzman, "The Portable Financial Analyst," *The Financial Analysts Journal* (Chicago: Irwin Professional Publishing, 1995), Chaps. 5 and 16.

experience, judgment, and common sense. In the end, the results must be something that both you and the client feel comfortable about.

III. Look on the bright side! There are advantages to the use of computer models. At least the model does not have to defend any turf. It has no ego to soothe, or any job security to worry about. It does what you and the designer tell it to do—nothing more, nothing less.

Different Design Methods

$\mathbf{Y}$ou say, "Okay, what do you use, Ron?" I use long-term history. I use APT results as an aid to investigate a possible structural change in the characteristics of an asset class. I look at a "most-likely" case. Then I perform a sensitivity analysis with a view of the best- and worst-case scenarios. Here are some other considerations.

GENERAL CONSIDERATIONS

CONSTANT OR VARIABLE?

The software used for illustrations in this book allows different expected returns for each year in the projection period. I have not found a method with which I feel comfortable to make productive use of this feature. For me, it is tough enough to produce an average expected return for each asset class for the 5-year measurement horizon.

RISK, CORRELATION COEFFICIENTS, AND AVERAGE YIELD

For better or for worse, I use long-term historical averages for these estimates.

MANAGEMENT FEES

I include our management fee in the calculation of target rate of return during the financial planning process. The expected return used in the optimizer is a gross figure. To do otherwise would be to double count fees. We do use this area of the model to input expected mutual fund fees such as manager fees, 12b-1 marketing fees, and other internal-cost items that make up the expense ratio.

TRANSACTION COSTS AND TURNOVER

It becomes important to take into account the practical cost associated with buying and selling securities within the mutual fund. It is equally important if there are brokerage costs associated with buying and selling the fund itself. Many fund supermarkets offer selected mutual funds with no transaction fees (NTF). Do not automatically assume that they are a better deal for the client. Was there a corre-sponding increase in the expense ratio over the shares of the same fund with no NTF? If so, the client may not be better off. Some mutual funds make a policy decision to cap their expense ratio at some maximum amount—for example, 1 percent. Another hidden cost here is the bid-ask spread. For funds offering small stocks, there could be a difference of from 6 to 8 percent between the bid and the ask price.

INCOME TAX BRACKET

Taxable portfolios have another major consideration for portfolio design, especially for clients in the top tax brackets. Optimizing a portfolio based on after-tax returns produces a different design than that of a tax-deferred portfolio.

CURRENCY OVERLAY

The accounts we oversee are in the United States and are denominated in dollars. Suppose that we had an offshore client, say, in Japan, and they place money in a U.S. account for me to oversee. They want me to design the portfolio to produce the optimum return in Yen, not U.S. dollars. Under those circumstances, the currency overlay feature would be important.

Another strategy comes from the use of hedging to take currency out of the equation. Michael Price does this with his international stock funds because he wants his return to reflect the fundamentals of the underlying securities.

HOLDING CONSTRAINTS

Individual

Refer to Figure 4–1, which shows the maximum or minimum constraints on the weighting assigned to any asset class. Constraints are usually the result of (1) client considerations or (2) portfolio considerations. The client may hold restricted stock with a contractual obligation not to sell for a period. There may be restrictions placed by the wording of a trust that bears on the client portfolio. The client may have a strong preference for or against a particular asset

F I G U R E 4–1

Individual Constraints

Individual Constraints		☒
Asset Class	**Min %**	**Max %**
Large Stocks	0.00%	100.00% ▲
Small Stocks	0.00%	100.00%
International Stocks	0.00%	100.00%
Emerging Countries	0.00%	100.00%
Intermediate Bonds	0.00%	100.00%
High Yield Bonds	0.00%	100.00%
Real Estate	0.00%	100.00%
Natural Resources	0.00%	100.00%
Short Term Bonds	0.00%	100.00%
Cash Equivalents	0.00%	100.00% ▼
	OK	**Cancel**

Software: Frontier Analytics, Inc., Investment Plus.

class. The client may require a minimum yield from an asset class or from the portfolio.

There can also be other considerations. An absence of any maximum constraint on asset classes can result in asset allocation to only two, perhaps even one, asset class. I find that clients are rarely comfortable with that notion. It is also a design not easily explained to a client. I typically put a maximum constraint of 25 percent of the portfolio on any asset class. That assures at least four asset classes. Some assets suggest a still shorter leash because of their volatility. "Emerging-country equities" is one example.

Sector Constraints

Refer to Figure 4–2. The word *sector* as used here refers to a grouping of asset classes. This has practical application if

FIGURE 4-2

Sector Constraints

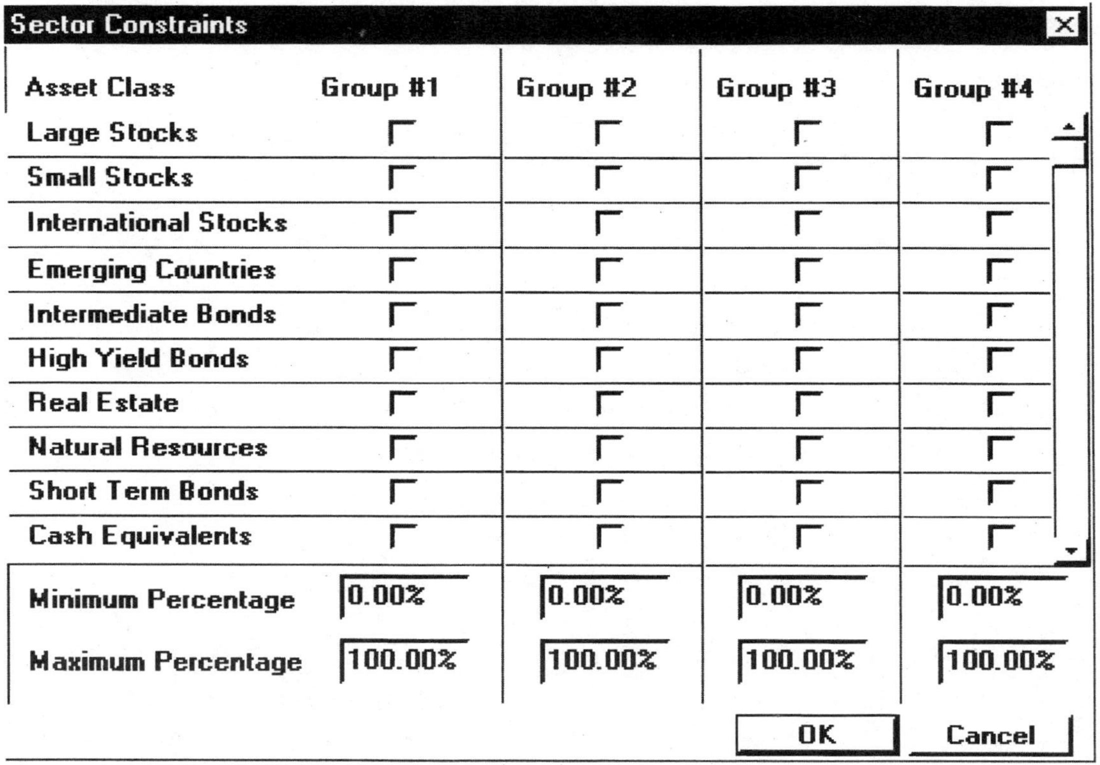

Sector Constraints

Asset Class	Group #1	Group #2	Group #3	Group #4
Large Stocks	L	L	L	L
Small Stocks	L	L	L	L
International Stocks	L	L	L	L
Emerging Countries	L	L	L	L
Intermediate Bonds	L	L	L	L
High Yield Bonds	L	L	L	L
Real Estate	L	L	L	L
Natural Resources	L	L	L	L
Short Term Bonds	L	L	L	L
Cash Equivalents	L	L	L	L
Minimum Percentage	0.00%	0.00%	0.00%	0.00%
Maximum Percentage	100.00%	100.00%	100.00%	100.00%

OK   Cancel

Software: Frontier Analytics, Inc., Investment Plus.

79

you want to put minimum or maximum constraints for one or more sectors. Your selection of asset classes may call for more than one fixed-income category. You also may wish to limit the overall exposure of fixed income to some percentage of the portfolio. You could do it here.

Intrasector Constraints
Refer to Figure 4–3. Let us say that the fixed-income sector consists of short-term bonds, intermediate-term bonds, and high-yield bonds. You could, for instance, limit the allocation of dollars to short-term bonds to no more than 5 percent of the fixed-income sector.

Portfolio Constraints
Refer to Figure 4–4. You and your client may wish to specify a minimum expected return, a maximum standard deviation, or a minimum yield constraint. In that case, the model considers only those combinations of assets that meet these constraints.

Tactical Ranges
Refer to Figure 4–5. Clients prefer not to be surprised. If you have discretion in the portfolio, the client may wish to know the rules that you apply to rebalancing their portfolio. This is the place to specify the percentage above or below target that triggers rebalancing.

CLIENT ASSETS

Present Asset Mix
Refer to Figure 4–6. Clients usually prefer to see a comparison of their current portfolio strategy with that suggested by the model. You can enter the weightings of asset classes

FIGURE 4-3

Intrasector Constraints

Intra-Sector Constraints   [X]

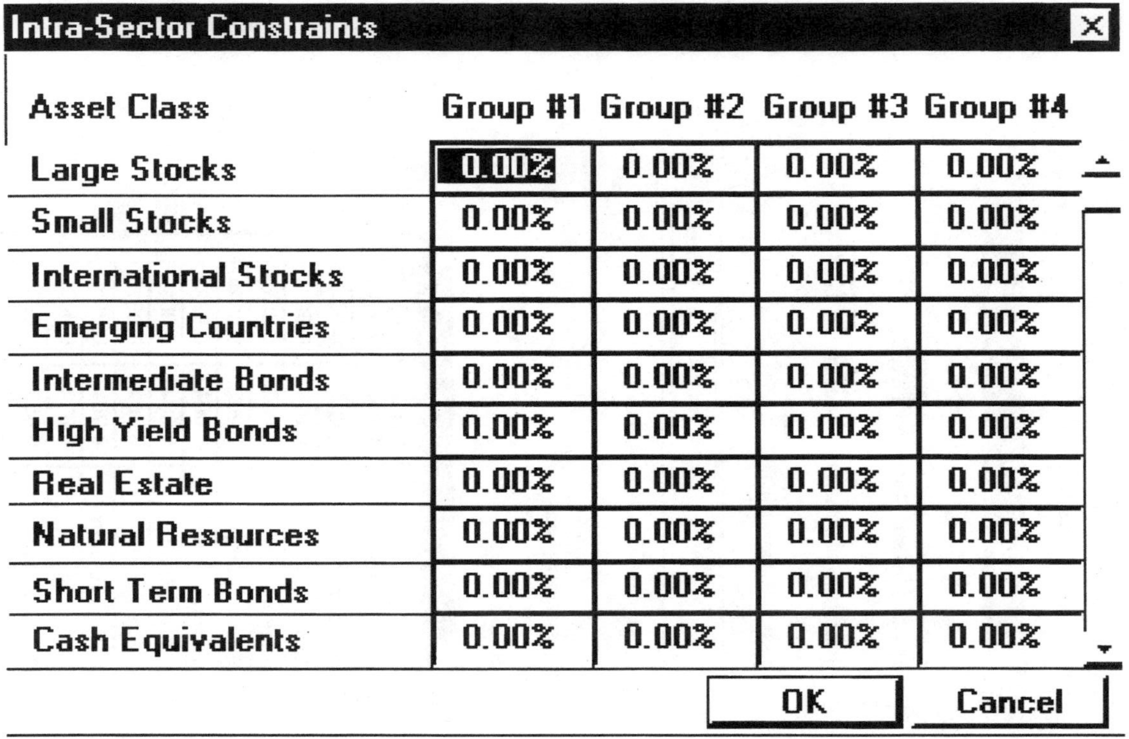

Asset Class	Group #1	Group #2	Group #3	Group #4
Large Stocks	0.00%	0.00%	0.00%	0.00%
Small Stocks	0.00%	0.00%	0.00%	0.00%
International Stocks	0.00%	0.00%	0.00%	0.00%
Emerging Countries	0.00%	0.00%	0.00%	0.00%
Intermediate Bonds	0.00%	0.00%	0.00%	0.00%
High Yield Bonds	0.00%	0.00%	0.00%	0.00%
Real Estate	0.00%	0.00%	0.00%	0.00%
Natural Resources	0.00%	0.00%	0.00%	0.00%
Short Term Bonds	0.00%	0.00%	0.00%	0.00%
Cash Equivalents	0.00%	0.00%	0.00%	0.00%

OK   Cancel

Software: Frontier Analytics, Inc., Investment Plus.

FIGURE 4–4

Portfolio Constraints

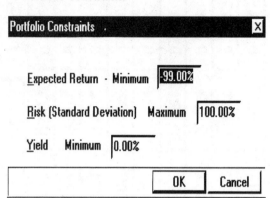

Software: Frontier Analytics, Inc., Investment Plus.

FIGURE 4–5

Tactical Limits

Asset Class	Below Target	Above Target
Large Stocks	0.00%	0.00%
Small Stocks	0.00%	0.00%
International Stocks	0.00%	0.00%
Emerging Countries	0.00%	0.00%
Intermediate Bonds	0.00%	0.00%
High Yield Bonds	0.00%	0.00%
Real Estate	0.00%	0.00%
Natural Resources	0.00%	0.00%
Short Term Bonds	0.00%	0.00%
Cash Equivalents	0.00%	0.00%

OK   Cancel

Software: Frontier Analytics, Inc., Investment Plus.

FIGURE 4-6

Present Asset Mix

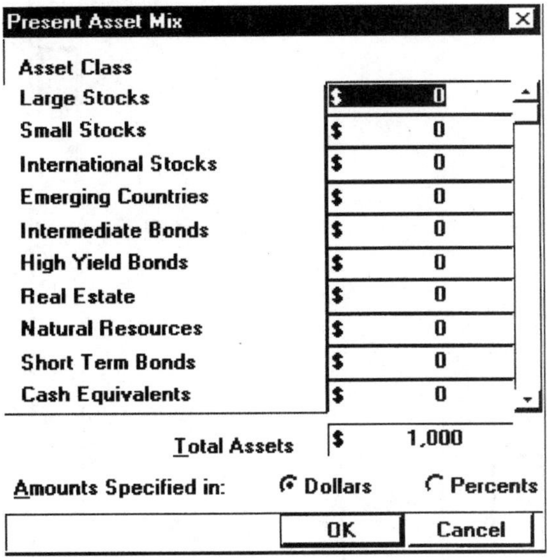

Present Asset Mix	
Asset Class	
Large Stocks	$ 0
Small Stocks	$ 0
International Stocks	$ 0
Emerging Countries	$ 0
Intermediate Bonds	$ 0
High Yield Bonds	$ 0
Real Estate	$ 0
Natural Resources	$ 0
Short Term Bonds	$ 0
Cash Equivalents	$ 0
Total Assets	$ 1,000
Amounts Specified in: ⦿ Dollars ⦾ Percents	
	OK Cancel

Software: Frontier Analytics, Inc., Investment Plus.

or the actual dollars allocated to the class. My preference is to use actual dollars. Clients have an easier time identifying with concrete dollars rather than abstract percentages.

Contributions or Cash Inflows

Refer to Figure 4–7. Your client may expect substantive cash inflows in the future. For instance, the client may plan to sell his or her business. He or she may wish to transfer the company retirement plan assets into a rollover IRA. This is the place to put these expected cash inflows.

FIGURE 4-7

Contributions or Cash Inflows

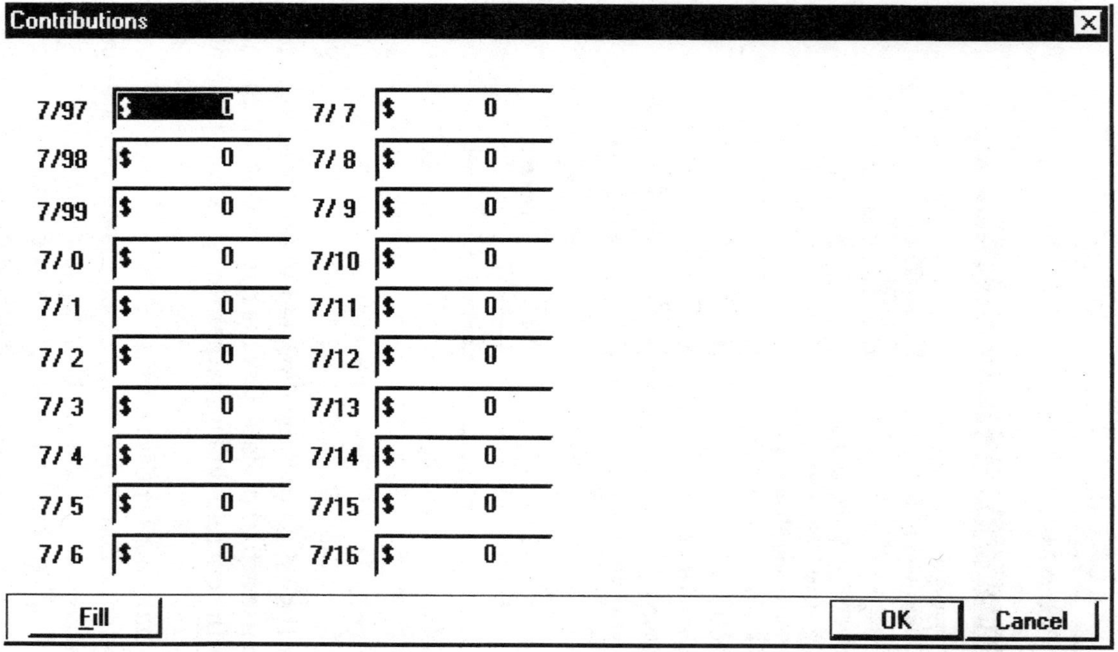

Contributions

7/97	$ 0	7/7	$ 0
7/98	$ 0	7/8	$ 0
7/99	$ 0	7/9	$ 0
7/0	$ 0	7/10	$ 0
7/1	$ 0	7/11	$ 0
7/2	$ 0	7/12	$ 0
7/3	$ 0	7/13	$ 0
7/4	$ 0	7/14	$ 0
7/5	$ 0	7/15	$ 0
7/6	$ 0	7/16	$ 0

Fill

OK   Cancel

Software: Frontier Analytics, Inc., Investment Plus.

Disbursements or Cash Outflows

Refer to Figure 4–8. The other side of the cash flow coin is planned substantive expenses. These are expenses requiring funding from portfolio assets. This might include lifestyle cash needs, an emergency buffer, charitable donations, gifts to family members, paying for college for grandchildren, or the financing of business interests. If you did not prepare a financial plan, here is the place to document those expenses.

OPTIMIZATION APPROACH: CUSTOMIZATION TO EACH CLIENT

There are three time horizons for consideration here. They are (1) *total planning horizon*, (2) *measurement horizon*, and (3) *portfolio review horizon*.

Total Planning Horizon

Refer to Figure 4–9. This covers the entire planning period for the strategic view. I typically use either 20 years or the life expectancy of the client. If the client is a couple, the life expectancy should be the longer of the two lives. The other periods shown on Figure 4–9 permit interim views of the total strategic plan period.

Measurement Horizon
(Optimization Time Horizon)

Refer to Figure 4–10. It is important to distinguish the measurement horizon from the total planning horizon. The total planning horizon consists of successive back-to-back increments of measurement horizons. The measurement horizon sets the client expectation about the minimum period over which the client should judge the performance of the advisor. I normally use 5 years for the measurement horizon, which should be enough time to cover a complete market

FIGURE 4-8

Disbursements or Cash Outflows

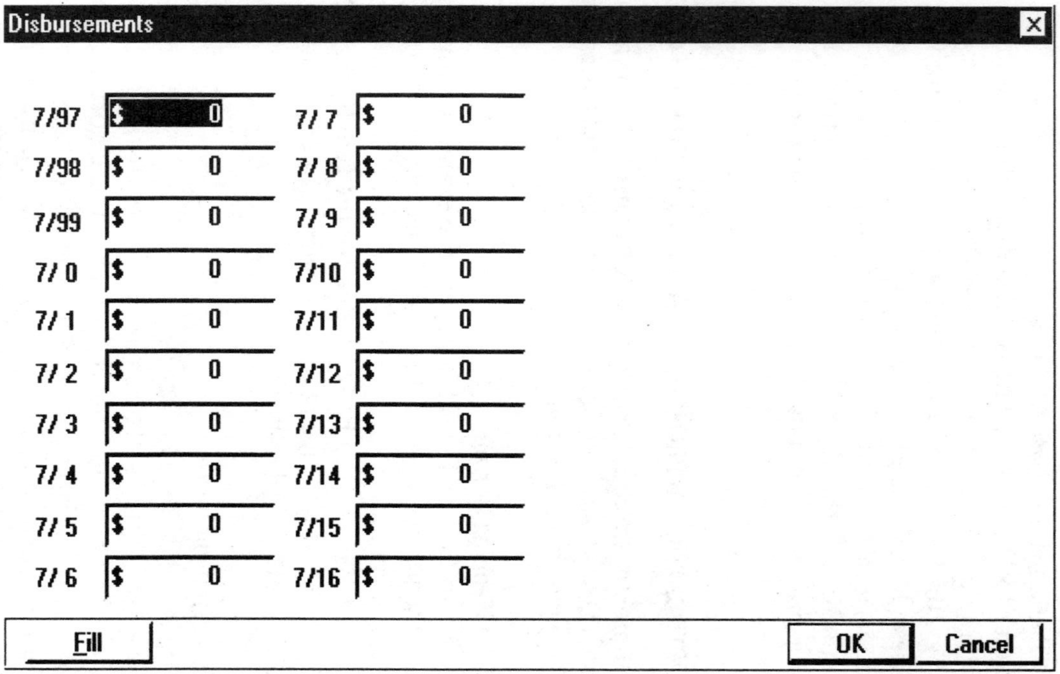

Software: Frontier Analytics, Inc., Investment Plus.

FIGURE 4-9

Total Planning Horizon

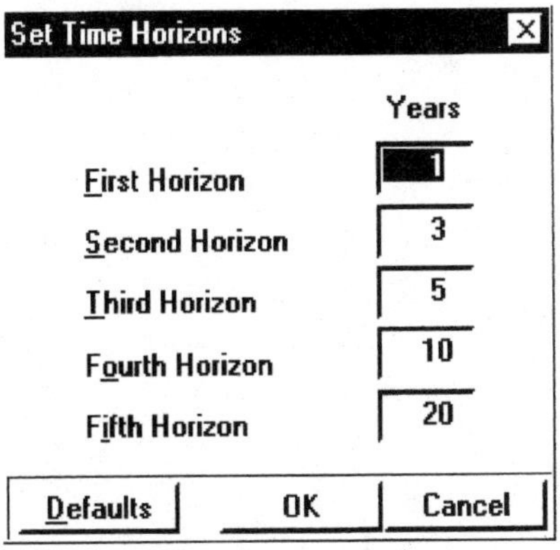

Software: Frontier Analytics, Inc., Investment Plus.

cycle. Placing a shorter period here (such as 1 year) can cause the model to suggest an allocation that varies significantly from year to year resulting in undue portfolio turnover. This can have adverse consequences for transaction costs for all portfolios. Even if you use funds with no-loads and no transaction fees, there are still income tax consequences for taxable portfolios.

Portfolio Review Horizon

It is also important to distinguish the time for periodic portfolio reviews from the 5-year measurement horizon. I normally conduct a formal portfolio review with the client once each year. If there is a major change in the client circumstances or assumptions that go into the model, I review the portfolio immediately. As part of that process, I run the

FIGURE 4-10

Optimization Method

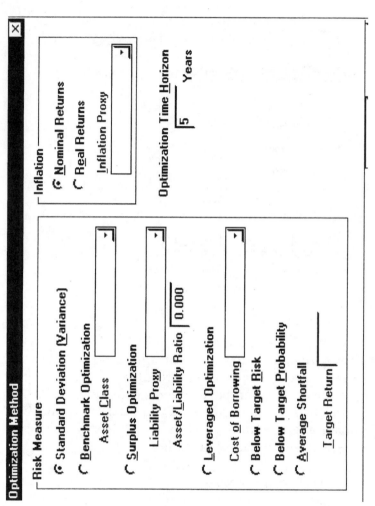

Software: Frontier Analytics, Inc., Investment Plus.

client asset allocation model to incorporate assumption changes. I keep the measurement horizon at 5 years.

Nominal or Real
Refer to Figure 4–10. Part of our role as an advisor is to educate the client about investing and investments. Running a model projection both before and after inflation is one important way to fulfill this role. When I calculate a target rate of return for a client, I consider inflation.

OPTIMIZATION METHODS FOR PRIVATE CLIENTS

There are several methods to optimize the portfolio, as shown in Figure 4–10. A brief discussion of each method follows.

MEAN-VARIANCE METHOD

Mean variance is the traditional Mean-Variance Optimization. Look at Figure 4–11. This is a picture of the standard deviation of actual monthly returns for 36-month rolling periods for the S&P 500 Stock Index. It covers the period from April 1994 through March 1997. The model used in this book[1] assumes a log-normal distribution of returns. So what? Using this log-normal approach gives a better fit than using a normal distribution. The results are closer to reality. I recognize that most of you reading this have not

---

1. Investment Plus, Frontier Analytics, Inc., 8910 University Center Lane, Suite 700, San Diego, CA 92122, phone (619) 552-1268.

FIGURE 4-11

S&P 500 Stock Index: Distribution of Returns

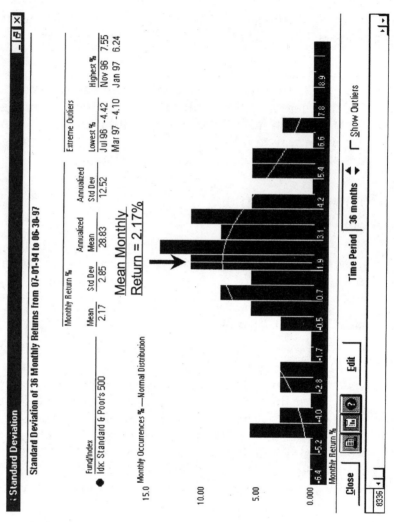

Source: Morningstar Principia Plus.

FIGURE 4–12

Specified Weightings: Stocks and Bonds

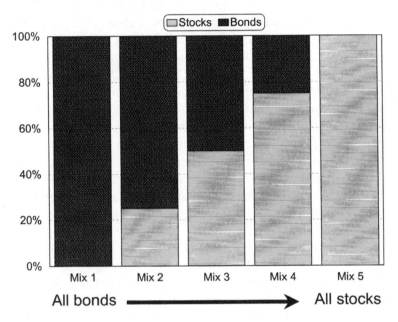

All bonds ➡ All stocks

dealt with logarithms in a while. If you want the details
about the math and the technical benefits of log-normal versus normal distributions, read Mark Kritzman's discussion.[2]

Two Asset Classes: Stocks and Bonds
Now look at Figure 4–12. Here I specified five portfolios
consisting of different mixtures of stocks and bonds. Now

2. Mark Kritzman, "The Portable Financial Analyst—What Practitioners Need to
   Know," *The Financial Analysts Journal* (Chicago: The Association for
   Investment Management and Research, Irwin Professional Publishing,
   1995), Chap. 4.

check Figure 4–13. This shows the distribution of returns for all five mixes for a 1-year holding period. The range shows what might happen for any year within the 20-year strategic view. What can we learn from this chart? You see five vertical bars. Keep in mind that Mix 1 is all bonds, and Mix 5 is all stocks. The 50th percentile line at the bottom of the page shows the mean return. The vertical bars show the mean return as the centerline drawn through the bar. The two lines on either side of the mean return show the 25th and 75th percentile lines. It says that there is a 50 percent chance for the return to be within this range. The top and bottom of each vertical bar show the 5th and 95th percentile lines. It says that there is a 90 percent chance for the return to be in this range. You may wish to consider the top and bottom of each bar as a fair representation of best and worst cases.

You can also see the skew in favor of positive returns from the log-normal assumption. As an example, for Mix 3 the difference between the mean (9.08 percent) and the 95th percentile (24.80 percent) is 15.72 percent. The difference between the mean and the 5th percentile (−4.66 percent) is 13.74 percent.

Note that all five mixes have a worst-case negative return for the 1-year holding period. I use a chart like this to provide an additional test of client risk tolerance. First, Mix 1 shows that a portfolio of all bonds has risk. Mix 2 shows, by adding some stocks to the blend, results in a reduced worst-case return over all bonds while increasing the average or mean return.

Now look at Figure 4–14. This is the same set of mixes, but after a 3-year holding period. Note that Mixes 2, 3, and 4 are all in the black even in the worst case. The degree to which Mixes 1 and 5 are negative is not significant.

Stocks and Bonds: 1-Year Holding Period

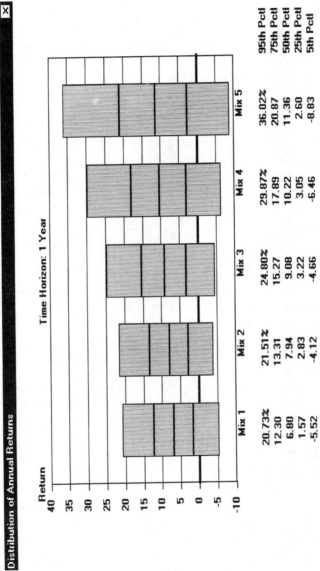

Distribution of Annual Returns

Time Horizon: 1 Year

	Mix 1	Mix 2	Mix 3	Mix 4	Mix 5	
	20.73%	21.51%	24.80%	29.87%	36.02%	95th Pctl
	12.30	13.31	15.27	17.89	20.87	75th Pctl
	6.80	7.94	9.08	10.22	11.36	50th Pctl
	1.57	2.83	3.22	3.05	2.60	25th Pctl
	-5.52	-4.12	-4.66	-6.46	-8.83	5th Pctl

Software: Frontier Analytics, Inc., Investment Plus.

93

FIGURE 4-14

Stocks and Bonds: 3-Year Holding Period

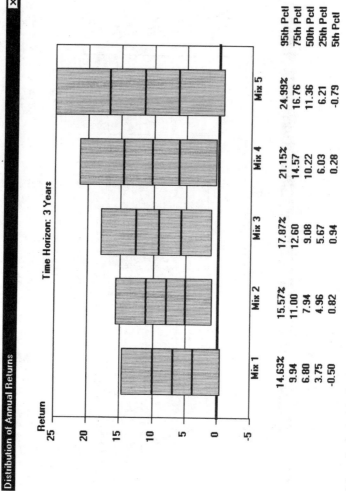

Distribution of Annual Returns

Time Horizon: 3 Years

Return	Mix 1	Mix 2	Mix 3	Mix 4	Mix 5	
	14.63%	15.57%	17.87%	21.15%	24.99%	95th Pctl
	9.94	11.00	12.60	14.57	16.76	75th Pctl
	6.80	7.94	9.08	10.22	11.36	50th Pctl
	3.75	4.96	5.67	6.03	6.21	25th Pctl
	-0.50	0.82	0.94	0.28	-0.79	5th Pctl

Software: Frontier Analytics, Inc., Investment Plus.

Figure 4–15 shows the same set of mixes after a 20-year holding period. Notice that the height of the vertical bars is less than that for shorter holding periods. That happens because the longer the holding period, the more the sum of positive and negative returns cancel each other out. Many refer to this as "time diversification." Some pundits question the time diversification assumption. For an objective view of both sides of the argument, read what Mark Kritzman has to say.[3] Markowitz also discusses this issue in his 1959 book *Portfolio Selection* that I referenced in Chapter 3.

Example of Mean-Variance Method

Let us consider an example of an optimization analysis using the mean-variance method. I assume that this is a qualified retirement plan or an IRA so that there is no immediate tax concern. The hypothetical client has a $1 million portfolio invested 60 percent in large stocks and 40 percent in intermediate-term bonds. Can we improve the productivity of this portfolio through higher return, lower risk, or a combination of both? Our target rate of return is 9 percent, our measurement time horizon is 5 years, use nominal returns, and limit the maximum allocation to each asset class of 25 percent.

Figure 4–16 shows the return and risk characteristics of the portfolios generated by the optimization model. This curve is the efficient frontier. Return increases up the vertical axis, and risk increases to the right on the horizontal

---

3. Ibid., Chap. 9.

FIGURE 4-15

Stocks and Bonds: 20-Year Holding Period

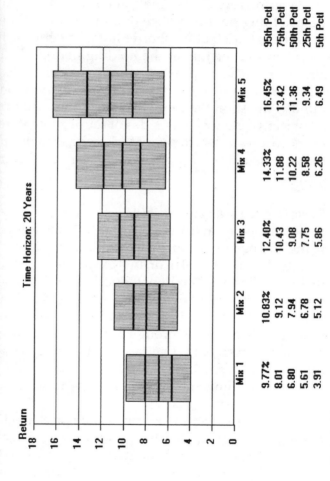

Distribution of Annual Returns

Time Horizon: 20 Years

	Mix 1	Mix 2	Mix 3	Mix 4	Mix 5	
	9.77%	10.83%	12.40%	14.33%	16.45%	95th Pctl
	8.01	9.12	10.43	11.88	13.42	75th Pctl
	6.80	7.94	9.08	10.22	11.36	50th Pctl
	5.61	6.78	7.75	8.58	9.34	25th Pctl
	3.91	5.12	5.86	6.26	6.49	5th Pctl

Software: Frontier Analytics, Inc., Investment Plus.

FIGURE 4-16

Mean-Variance Method: Efficient Frontier

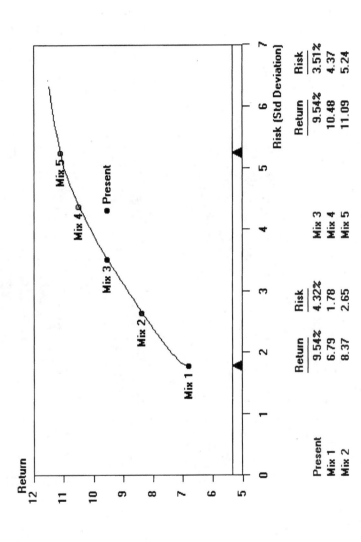

Efficient Frontier ☒

	Return	Risk
Present	9.54%	4.32%
Mix 1	6.79	1.78
Mix 2	8.37	2.65

	Return	Risk
Mix 3	9.54%	3.51%
Mix 4	10.48	4.37
Mix 5	11.09	5.24

Software: Frontier Analytics, Inc., Investment Plus.

FIGURE 4-17

Mean-Variance Method: Asset Class Weighting

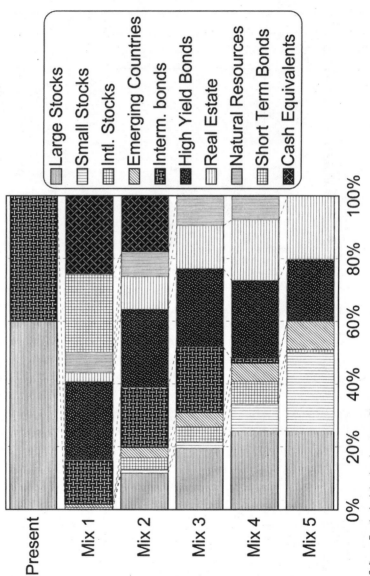

Software: Frontier Analytics, Inc., Investment Plus.

axis. Remember that standard deviation of returns is the measurement of risk in the mean-variance method. Notice that the present portfolio is not on the efficient frontier curve. In other words, there is a higher and better use of the $1 million than a mix of 60 percent large stocks and 40 percent intermediate-term bonds.

Figure 4–17 shows the asset weightings of the present portfolio and the five "mix" portfolios. Figure 4–18 shows the asset weighting for Mix 3. Notice that this chart includes a number at the bottom referred to as the *Sharpe ratio*, which is a measure of portfolio productivity. It is a quotient having excess return over the risk-free rate as the numerator and the standard deviation of returns as the denominator. There is a discussion by Dr. Sharpe of the details of this measurement and its appropriate use in *The Journal of Portfolio Management*.[4]

Figure 4–19 shows a continuum of asset class weightings along the efficient frontier. For any level of return you can see the asset class weighting. Figure 4–20 shows a similar continuum of asset class weightings. In this case, the horizontal axis shows increasing risk. Figure 4–21 shows the range of returns for a 1-year holding period. Notice that only the most aggressive strategy, Mix 5, has a higher worst-case return than the present case. Figure 4–22 shows the distribution of annual returns for Mix 3 versus the present mix. Note that Mix 3 produces the same return as the present mix but with less risk or volatility.

I find that many clients have an *intuitive* if not an *analytical* understanding of probabilities. Analogies seem to

---

4. William F. Sharpe, "The Sharpe Ratio," *The Journal of Portfolio Management*, vol. 21, no. 1, Fall 1994.

FIGURE 4-18

Mean-Variance Method: Mix 3 Characteristics

Mix Characteristics: Mix 3

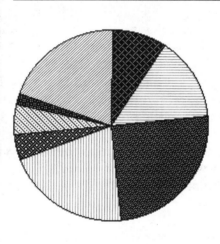

Large Stocks	20%
Small Stocks	2
International Stocks	5
Emerging Countries	4
Intermediate Bonds	21
High Yield Bonds	24
Real Estate	14
Natural Resources	10

Return: 9.54%
Standard Deviation: 3.51%
Yield: 5.38%
Sharpe Ratio: 1.49

Software: Frontier Analytics, Inc., Investment Plus.

F I G U R E 4–19

Mean-Variance Method: Asset Class Weighting Versus Return

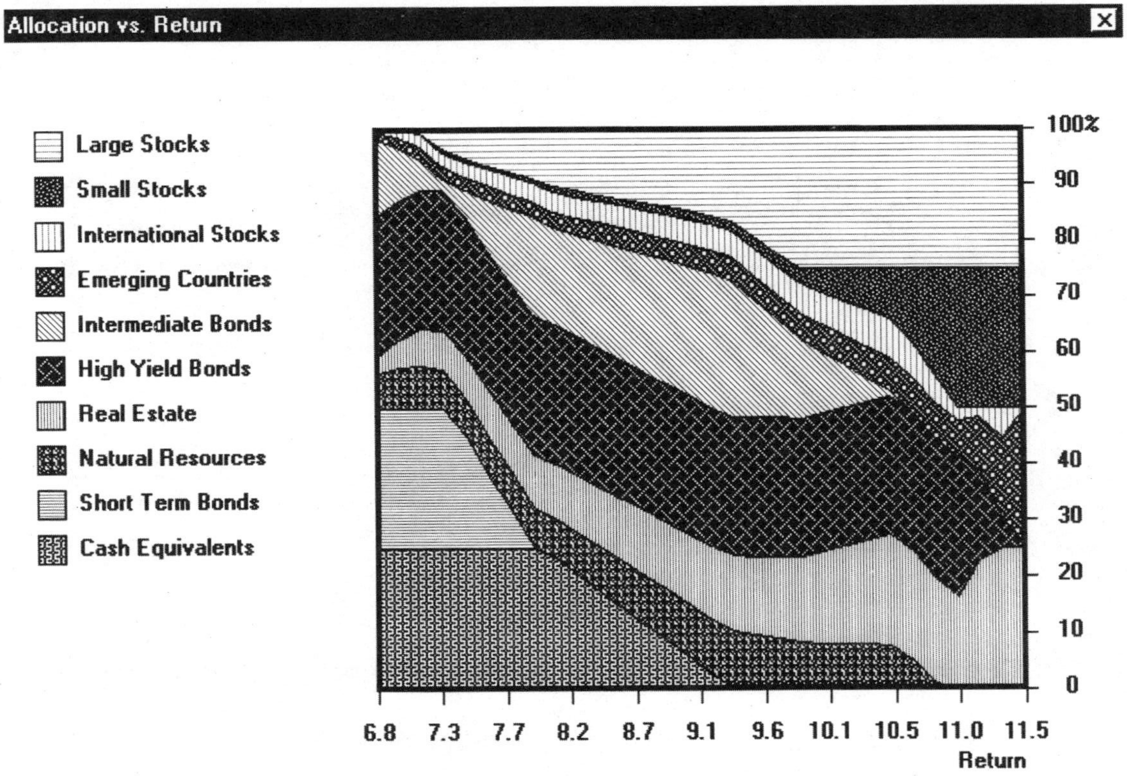
Allocation vs. Return
Large Stocks
Small Stocks
International Stocks
Emerging Countries
Intermediate Bonds
High Yield Bonds
Real Estate
Natural Resources
Short Term Bonds
Cash Equivalents
100%
90
80
70
60
50
40
30
20
10
0
6.8
7.3
7.7
8.2
8.7
9.1
9.6
10.1
10.5
11.0
11.5
Return

Software: Frontier Analytics, Inc., Investment Plus.

FIGURE 4–20

Mean-Variance Method: Asset Class Weighting Versus Risk

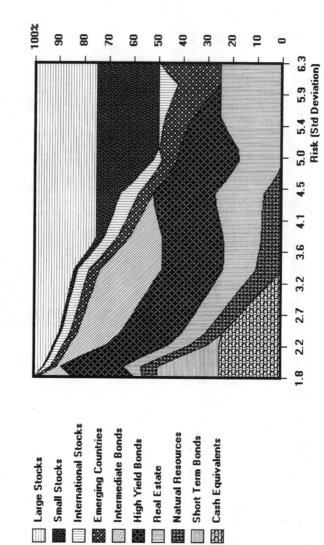

Allocation vs. Risk [X]

- Large Stocks
- Small Stocks
- International Stocks
- Emerging Countries
- Intermediate Bonds
- High Yield Bonds
- Real Estate
- Natural Resources
- Short Term Bonds
- Cash Equivalents

Software: Frontier Analytics, Inc., Investment Plus.

Mean-Variance Method: Present and Five Suggested Mixes, 1-Year Holding Period

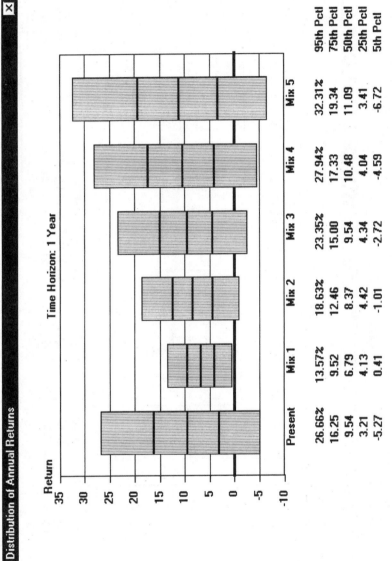

Distribution of Annual Returns

Time Horizon: 1 Year

	Present	Mix 1	Mix 2	Mix 3	Mix 4	Mix 5	
	26.66%	13.57%	18.63%	23.35%	27.94%	32.31%	95th Pctl
	16.25	9.52	12.46	15.00	17.33	19.34	75th Pctl
	9.54	6.79	8.37	9.54	10.48	11.09	50th Pctl
	3.21	4.13	4.42	4.34	4.04	3.41	25th Pctl
	-5.27	0.41	-1.01	-2.72	-4.59	-6.72	5th Pctl

Software: Frontier Analytics, Inc., Investment Plus.

FIGURE 4-22

Mean-Variance Method: Present Versus Mix 3— 1-, 3-, 5-, 10-, and 20-Year Holding Periods

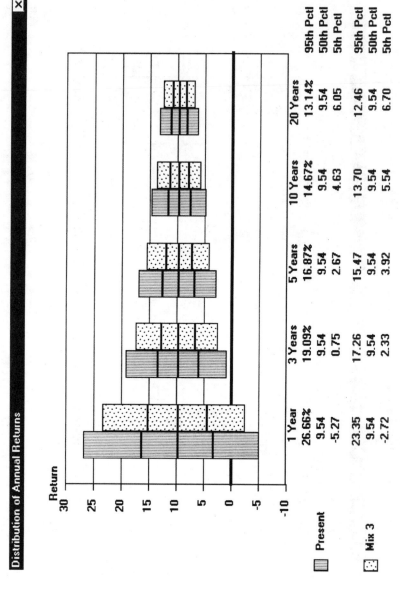

Distribution of Annual Returns

	1 Year	3 Years	5 Years	10 Years	20 Years	
	26.66%	19.09%	16.87%	14.67%	13.14%	95th Pctl
	9.54	9.54	9.54	9.54	9.54	50th Pctl
	-5.27	0.75	2.67	4.63	6.05	5th Pctl
	23.35	17.26	15.47	13.70	12.46	95th Pctl
	9.54	9.54	9.54	9.54	9.54	50th Pctl
	-2.72	2.33	3.92	5.54	6.70	5th Pctl

Present

Mix 3

Software: Frontier Analytics, Inc., Investment Plus.

help the communication process. For example, in crucial situations, a baseball manager prefers to have a hitter with a *high batting average* at the plate. The *chance* of driving in a run is higher with the better hitter. Some clients may not have familiarity with the nuances of baseball. All is not lost. They may be familiar with the *odds* associated with various tables at a gambling casino. (Rule 1: The house always gets theirs. Rule 2: Do not forget rule 1.)

Figure 4–23 is an example of probability math applied to the results of our optimization projections. It is a graphical representation of the chance of the Mix 3 portfolio either (1) not losing money (exceeding 0 percent), (2) exceeding 5 percent, or (3) exceeding the target return of 9 percent. Before you try to explain this to a client, you may want to refresh your understanding of probability theory. Most college-level books on statistics have a chapter or two on this subject.

BENCHMARK METHOD

Your client may prefer to think about a portfolio return exceeding some benchmark index. In this case, one must think in terms of a trade-off between *excess return* (return greater than the benchmark) and a statistical measurement of risk known as *tracking error*. Tracking error analysis has some similarities with mean-variance analysis. It too assumes a bell-shaped curve, and it involves the calculation of mean, standard deviation, and degrees of freedom. Tracking error is a mathematical representation of the degree to which the portfolio behavior mirrors the benchmark behavior.

Refer back to Figure 4–10. The section labeled "benchmark optimization" permits this type of analysis. For example, your client wants the behavior of the portfolio under

FIGURE 4-23

Mean-Variance Method: Mix 3, Probability of Exceeding 0 Percent, 5 Percent, and 9 Percent

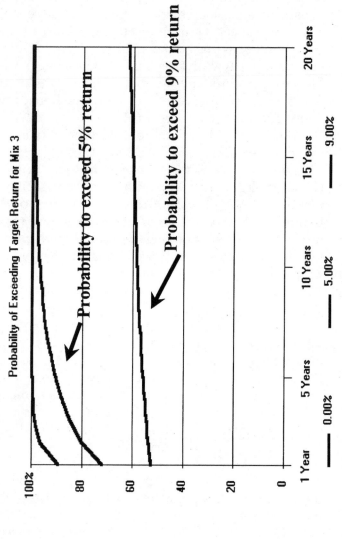

Software: Frontier Analytics, Inc., Investment Plus.

design to meet and preferably exceed that of our asset class labeled "intermediate-term bonds." To do this, you select the "benchmark optimization method" as shown in Figure 4-10. You select intermediate bonds as the benchmark.

Optimization produces an efficient frontier graph like Figure 4–24. Compare it with mean variance in Figure 4–16. On the vertical axis, you see "excess return" instead of "total return." On the horizontal axis, you see "tracking error" instead of "standard deviation." Figure 4–25 shows a continuum along the efficient frontier and a suggested asset class weighting versus different excess returns. Figure 4–26 shows suggested asset class weighting versus increasing tracking error. In this example, the asset class "intermediate bonds" does not appear in the analysis since it is the standard of measurement.

BELOW-TARGET-RISK METHOD

In the sixteenth century, the astronomer Copernicus advanced the theory that the earth and other planets revolve around the sun. In the following century, another astronomer named Galileo advocated the theories of Copernicus. This idea was out of step with the mainstream thinking of Galileo's time, and it led to his persecution and imprisonment in 1633.

That is very interesting, but what is the point? The point is this: The theory discussed next is not in step with most "mainstream" thinking of today. It is different from MVO and CAPM. It is, however, in my judgment, a serious idea worthy of your consideration. It advances the state of the art in portfolio design. Even so, please note Markowitz's comment about this technique discussed in Chapter 3. He said in effect that proof that the below-target-risk method is better than MVO does not yet exist. I find one clear advan-

FIGURE 4-24

Benchmark Optimization Method: Benchmark—Intermediate-Term Bonds

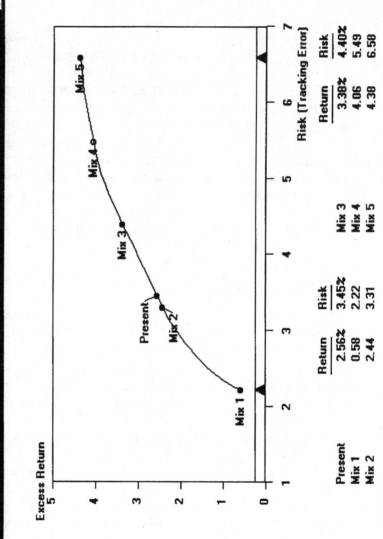

Software: Frontier Analytics, Inc., Investment Plus.

FIGURE 4-25

Benchmark Optimization Method: Benchmark—Intermediate-Term Bonds, Allocation Versus Excess Return

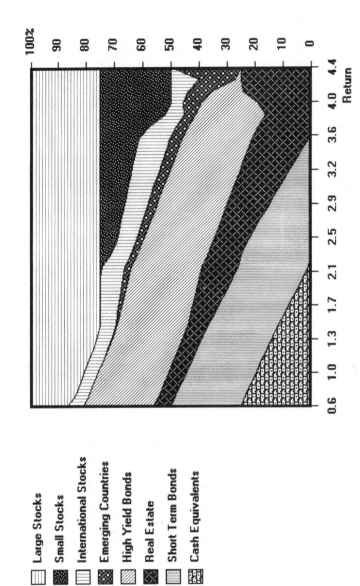

Allocation vs. Return

Large Stocks
Small Stocks
International Stocks
Emerging Countries
High Yield Bonds
Real Estate
Short Term Bonds
Cash Equivalents

Software: Frontier Analytics, Inc., Investment Plus.

FIGURE 4-26

Benchmark Optimization Method: Benchmark—Intermediate-Term Bonds, Allocation Versus Tracking Error (Risk)

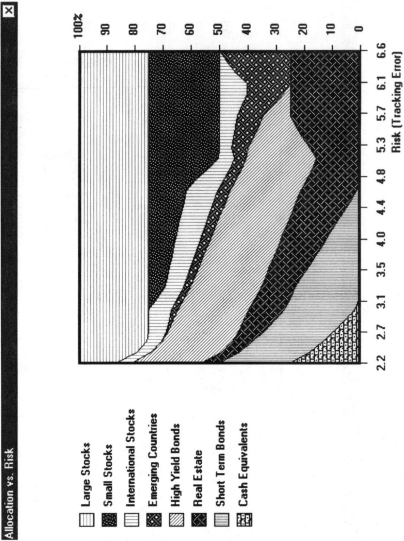

Allocation vs. Risk

Large Stocks
Small Stocks
International Stocks
Emerging Countries
High Yield Bonds
Real Estate
Short Term Bonds
Cash Equivalents

Software: Frontier Analytics, Inc., Investment Plus.

tage with semivariance. My clients seem to identify with the underlying rationale better than they do with MVO.

Let me start with a hypothetical example. Let us assume that you are an investment advisor designing a portfolio with a private client. Suppose you say, "Investment risk is the variation of investment returns above and below the average return for that investment." You say, "A large negative return below the average return is bad." Your client nods in agreement.

Then you say, "Large positive returns above the average are equally bad." The body language of your client changes dramatically. You see a puzzled look come over his or her face. Your client folds his or her arms and says, "You must be joking!" You go on. "In addition, we assume that negative returns occur just as often as positive returns." Your client knows from experience what any schoolchild knows. The market is up more often than it is down by a sizeable margin. At this point, the body language of your client changes again. With a concerned look, your client asks, "Are you sure you feel okay?"

Is this vignette too dramatic? Perhaps it is. At least you get the point. This is the practical dilemma faced by any advisor trying to explain MVO to a client. The use of standard deviation is simply counterintuitive to the layperson.

Enter, from stage right, semivariance or downside risk. Who do you suppose first introduced this topic to investment theory? It was Harry Markowitz [1959]. Chapter 9 and a portion of the appendix of his 1959 book cover this topic. Markowitz felt then, as he does now, that semivariance is no better than MVO. The topic next appeared in 1977 in an article by Peter Fishburn.[5] Fishburn referred to his theory as

5. Peter Fishburn, "Mean-Risk Analysis with Risk Associated with Below-Market Returns," *American Economic Review*, March 1977.

"Mean Lower Partial Moment." Downside risk accounts for *asymmetry* in return distributions. Statisticians refer to *skewness* and *kurtosis*. These terms provide a mathematical description of these properties. Another advocate of downside risk is Dr. Frank Sortino. He is the director of the Pension Research Institute and Professor Emeritus of Finance from San Francisco State University. He writes a regular column in *Pensions and Investments*. His first article about downside risk came in 1980.[6]

A more recent article by Sortino appears in *The Journal of Investing*.[7] He discusses the minimum return required by an investor to achieve his or her goals. He refers to this as the *minimum acceptable return*, or MAR. Any return below this MAR is an unfavorable outcome and is defined as risk. Thus, MAR separates "good volatility" from "bad volatility." The more the return is below the MAR, the greater the risk. The calculation of "below target variance" makes use of integral calculus. "Below target risk" is the square root of below target variance. This has a parallel in MVO, in which standard deviation is the square root of variance. The Sortino ratio measures the productivity of the portfolio for any asset mix. In the numerator, there is the difference between the expected return and the MAR; the denominator has the downside risk. It has a parallel in the Sharpe ratio.

Figure 4–27 shows an efficient frontier calculated with the below-target-risk method. It assumes a target return

6. Frank A. Sortino and David Hopelain, "The Pension Fund: Investment or Capital Budgeting Decision?" *Financial Executive,* August 1980.
7. Frank A. Sortino and Lee N. Price, "Performance Measurement in a Downside Risk Framework," *The Journal of Investing,* vol. 3, no. 3, Fall 1994.

FIGURE 4-27

Below-Target-Risk Method: Specified Minimum Return of 9 Percent

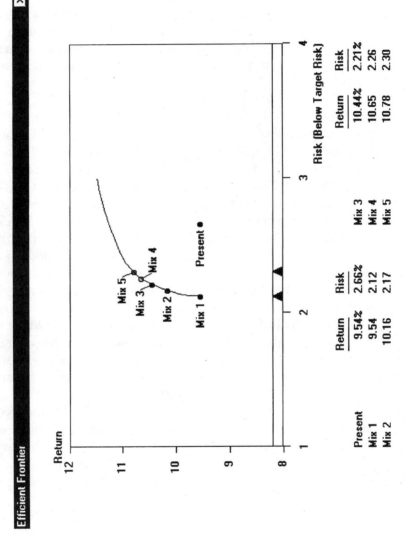

Efficient Frontier ☒

	Return	Risk
Present	9.54%	2.66%
Mix 1	9.54	2.12
Mix 2	10.16	2.17

	Return	Risk
Mix 3	10.44%	2.21%
Mix 4	10.65	2.26
Mix 5	10.78	2.30

Software: Frontier Analytics, Inc., Investment Plus.

(minimum acceptable return, or MAR) of 9 percent. Note that the measurement on the horizontal axis is below target risk. Figure 4–28 shows the content of Mixes 1 through 5. You can also see there a comparison of the calculated values of standard deviation, below target risk, Sharpe ratio, and Sortino ratio.

Brian Rom and Kathleen Ferguson also made significant contributions to the downside-risk discussion. They published an article titled "Post-Modern Portfolio Theory Comes of Age."[8] While it may be a bit premature to declare the death of MVO and CAPM, the authors do have many constructive and useful things to say about downside risk. For example, they say that the downside-risk calculation produces an efficient frontier unique to each client MAR. You can split the downside-risk statistic into two components. They are *downside probability* and *average downside magnitude.* Downside probability measures the likelihood of failure to meet the MAR. The average downside magnitude measures the average shortfall below the MAR. The calculation includes only those instances when the MAR is not achieved. You can think of it as a measure of the consequences of failure. In the interests of full disclosure, Rom and Ferguson are principals in a firm that markets software that uses "Post MPT" methodology.

My opinion is that downside risk has an intuitive look and feel not present with standard deviation. Clients seem to "tune in" much quicker with it than they do with standard deviation. Only time will tell if downside risk is truly Post-Modern Portfolio Theory. This is a call for some bright

---

8. Brian M. Rom and Kathleen W. Ferguson, "Post-Modern Portfolio Theory Comes of Age," *The Journal of Investing,* vol. 3, no. 3, Fall 1994.

Below-Target-Risk Method: Specified Minimum Return of 9 Percent

Investment Alternatives ☒

Asset Class	Present	Mix 1	Mix 2	Mix 3	Mix 4	Mix 5
Large Stocks	60.00%	19.46%	25.00%	25.00%	25.00%	25.00%
Small Stocks	0.00	2.04	5.58	8.21	12.69	17.35
International Stocks	0.00	4.87	6.20	7.07	6.59	5.50
Emerging Countries	0.00	4.40	5.22	5.75	6.08	6.25
Intermediate Bonds	40.00	20.91	8.00	2.21	0.00	0.00
High Yield Bonds	0.00	25.00	25.00	25.00	25.00	25.00
Real Estate	0.00	13.88	17.12	19.12	19.46	18.90
Natural Resources	0.00	9.44	7.88	7.63	5.18	2.01
Short Term Bonds	0.00	0.00	0.00	0.00	0.00	0.00
Cash Equivalents	0.00	0.00	0.00	0.00	0.00	0.00
Return	9.54%	9.54%	10.16%	10.44%	10.65%	10.78%
Std Deviation	4.32%	3.51%	4.05%	4.33%	4.55%	4.72%
Yield	4.52%	5.38%	4.97%	4.78%	4.71%	4.71%
Sharpe Ratio	1.21	1.49	1.44	1.42	1.39	1.37
Below Target Risk	2.66%	2.12%	2.17%	2.21%	2.26%	2.30%
Sortino Ratio	0.20	0.25	0.54	0.65	0.73	0.78
Target Return	9.00%					
Time Horizon	5					

Software: Frontier Analytics, Inc., Investment Plus.

115

Ph.D. student to choose a dissertation with a focus on an objective, analytical study of MVO versus semivariance. I hope that someone is listening out there!

Frank Sortino also offers a word of caution about the calculation of downside risk.[9] He says that some practitioners calculate it using a "discrete" distribution of monthly returns. Dr. Sortino says that this method does not offer sufficient precision and can give misleading results. Thus, the discrete method has flaws. Instead, Sortino suggests use of a continuous distribution using integral calculus. The software used in this book to produce downside-risk illustrations follows Dr. Sortino's recommendations.

You can limit mean-variance portfolios to returns that meet or exceed the MAR of the client. Refer back to Figure 4–4. There you see a panel allowing specification of a minimum expected return. You can think of this as the equivalent of the MAR. Using a Mean-Variance Optimization Method and a 9 percent MAR specification produces an efficient frontier as shown in Figure 4–29. Everything is the same as Figure 4-16 except the model confines the choices on the frontier to those that meet or exceed the MAR of 9 percent. Note that Mix 1 has an expected return of 9 percent. Mix 2 has a return of 9.54 percent, the same as the present portfolio. Mixes 3, 4, and 5 returns all exceed the return of the present portfolio. Figure 4–30 shows the details of the calculation. You may wish to compare this table with the one in Figure 4–28.

Remember that the risk shown in Figures 4–29 and 4–30 is our old friend standard deviation with "good risk"

---

9. Frank A. Sortino and Hal J. Forsey, "On the Use and Misuse of Downside Risk," *The Journal of Portfolio Management*, Winter 1996.

FIGURE 4–29

Mean-Variance Method: Specified Minimum Return of 9 Percent

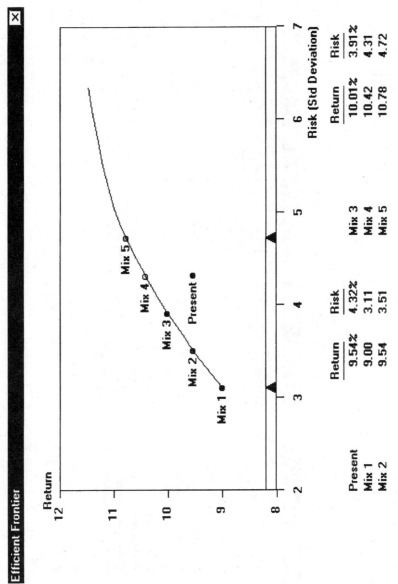

Efficient Frontier

	Return	Risk		Return	Risk
Present	9.54%	4.32%	Mix 3	10.01%	3.91%
Mix 1	9.00	3.11	Mix 4	10.42	4.31
Mix 2	9.54	3.51	Mix 5	10.78	4.72

Software: Frontier Analytics, Inc., Investment Plus.

F I G U R E 4–30

Mean-Variance Method: Specified Minimum Return of 9 Percent

Investment Alternatives ☒

Asset Class	Present	Mix 1	Mix 2	Mix 3	Mix 4	Mix 5
Large Stocks	60.00%	14.48%	19.42%	25.00%	25.00%	25.00%
Small Stocks	0.00	1.42	2.04	4.16	8.07	17.24
International Stocks	0.00	4.32	4.87	5.73	7.02	5.53
Emerging Countries	0.00	3.89	4.40	4.93	5.72	6.24
Intermediate Bonds	40.00	22.98	20.95	11.13	2.54	0.00
High Yield Bonds	0.00	25.00	25.00	25.00	25.00	25.00
Real Estate	0.00	12.25	13.88	16.03	19.01	18.91
Natural Resources	0.00	9.37	9.45	8.01	7.64	2.08
Short Term Bonds	0.00	0.00	0.00	0.00	0.00	0.00
Cash Equivalents	0.00	6.30	0.00	0.00	0.00	0.00
Return	9.54%	9.00%	9.54%	10.01%	10.42%	10.78%
Std Deviation	4.32%	3.11%	3.51%	3.91%	4.31%	4.72%
Yield	4.52%	5.50%	5.39%	5.08%	4.79%	4.71%
Sharpe Ratio	1.21	1.51	1.49	1.46	1.42	1.37

Software: Frontier Analytics, Inc., Investment Plus.

and "bad risk" treated with equal disdain. I do not mean to suggest that the mathematics used to produce the frontier in Figure 4–29 is a rigorous substitute for downside risk. What I show here is an adaptation of the Mean-Variance Method designed to answer *some* of the criticisms leveled by the advocates of downside risk. Those adaptations include the assumption of MAR and a log-normal distribution of returns that provides a natural positive "tilt"[10] of returns.

Morningstar is a leading publisher of mutual fund information. They also adopted the downside-risk concept and applied it to the mutual fund analysis they publish. Here is Morningstar's definition of downside risk as they use it:

Morningstar Risk

Listed for 3, 5, and 10 years, a statistic that evaluates the funds downside volatility relative to that of others in its investment class. To calculate risk, Morningstar concentrates on those months during which a fund underperformed the average return of a three-month Treasury bill. We add up the amounts by which the fund fell short of the Treasury bills return and divide the result by the total number of months in the rating period. The funds average monthly loss is then compared with the average monthly loss for the funds investment class. The resulting risk rating expresses how risky the fund is, relative to the average fund in the investment class. Since the average risk rating for the funds investment class is 1.00, a Morningstar risk rating of 1.35 for a taxable-bond fund reveals that the fund has been

---

10. *Tilt* is a highly technical term, and its definition is beyond the scope of this text.

35 percent riskier than the average taxable-bond fund for the period considered.[11]

Benefits

Morningstar uses a proprietary risk measure that operates differently from traditional risk measures, such as beta and standard deviation, which see both greater- and less-than-expected returns as added volatility. Morningstar believes the risk of investing in a particular fund lies in the potential that it will perform worse than other investment options such as a risk-free treasury bill.

Origin

Morningstar generates this statistic in-house:

Example

Benham GNMA Income fund has a 3-year Risk score of .71 , a 5-year Risk score of .73, and a weighted average Risk score of .72. The average for the class being set at 1.00, Benham GNMA Income has consistently incurred a lower risk (on average by 28 percent) than its peers.

This calculation by Morningstar might not pass the mathematical rigor test of Dr. Sortino. It does, however, make intuitive sense. The Morningstar definition also does not speak to individual client target rate of return or MAR. I use Morningstar Risk when I discuss the funds I have selected for my clients. (Yes, I discuss standard deviation with them also. No, it is not as bad as my little vignette that I presented earlier.)

---

11. *Source:* Morningstar Principia Plus for Mutual Funds.

Passive Investing—It's Not Just Academic

WHAT IS ALL THE EXCITEMENT ABOUT?

Please focus your attention on Figures 5–1 and 5–2. These pictures make it clear why indexing has received so much attention lately, mainly from investors and the media. The fund is the patriarch, or matriarch, if you like, of index funds. It is the Vanguard Index 500, and it is a picture of the returns and an expression of demand for the fund shares over the last few years. The proxy for demand is the increase in the size of the fund. Note that the total returns for 1995 and 1996 were 37.45 and 22.86 percent, respectively. That exceeds the returns of 88 percent of the domestic Diversified Equity Funds for 1995 and 79 percent for 1996. The extraordinary level of demand makes this fund currently number 1 in terms of growth in dollar volume. Figure 5-2 shows the total size of the fund year by year. As

FIGURE 5-1

Vanguard Index 500: Percent Change in Assets, Percent Total Return

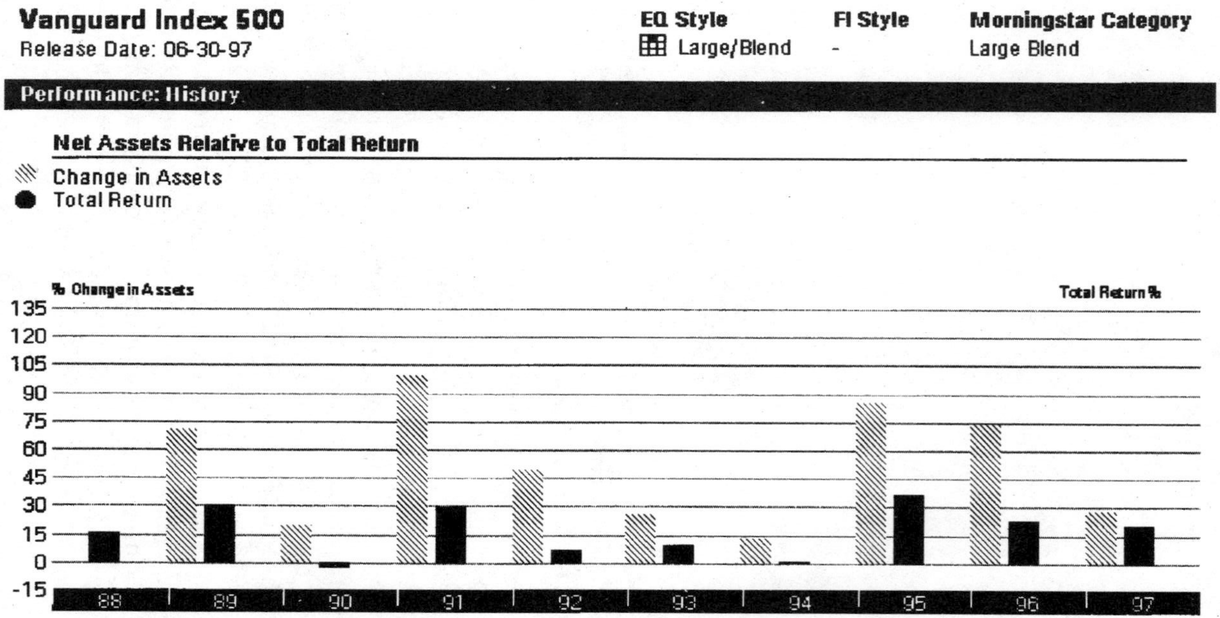

Vanguard Index 500
Release Date: 06-30-97

EQ Style
Large/Blend

FI Style
-

Morningstar Category
Large Blend

Performance: History

Net Assets Relative to Total Return

Change in Assets
Total Return

% Change in Assets

135
120
105
90
75
60
45
30
15
0
-15

88 89 90 91 92 93 94 95 96 97

Total Return %

Data Source: Morningstar Principia.

FIGURE 5-2

Vanguard Index 500: Size of Fund, $

Vanguard Index 500
Release Date: 03-31-97

EQ Style
Large/Blend

FI Style
-

Objective
Growth and Income

Performance: History

Net Assets

Vanguard Index 500

Current Net Assets ($mil)

34587

Net Assets ($mil)

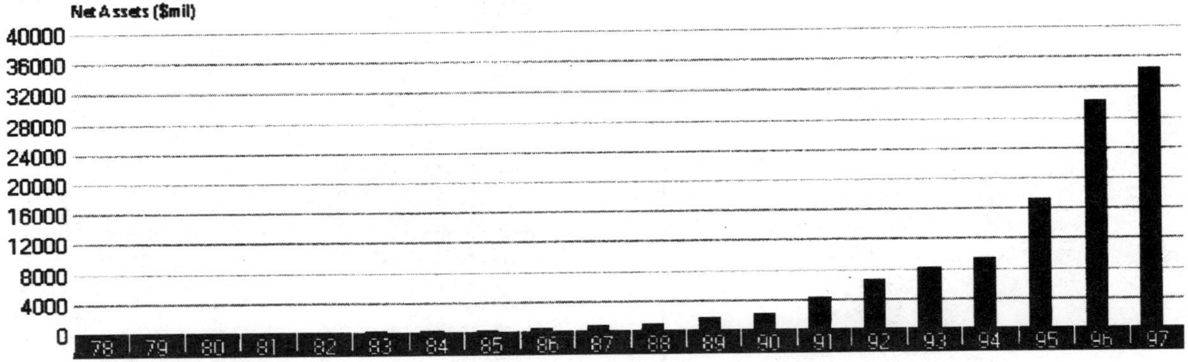

Data Source: Morningstar Principia.

123

I write this, the Vanguard Index 500 Fund is second in size
only to Fidelity Magellan. The typical index investor asks,
"Why should I spend my time pouring over fund information when I can just buy an index fund and forget it?"

A LOOK AT THE BIG PICTURE

Look at Figure 5–3. It shows the percentile rank of the
Vanguard Index 500 Fund among the diversified Domestic
Equity Funds. There are 266 funds shown here with a
record of accomplishment at least as long as the Vanguard

FIGURE 5–3

Vanguard Index 500: Rank within 266 U.S. Diversified Equity Funds

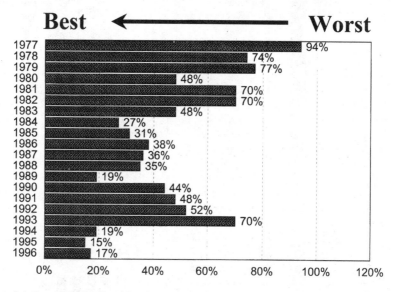

Data Source: ValueLine Mutual Fund Survey for Windows.

Index 500. There you see that the Vanguard 500 was in the 17th percentile in 1996 and the 15th percentile in 1995. Things were not always as upbeat for the Vanguard Index 500 Fund. Look at 1993 and the period from 1977 through 1982. Returns in those periods are less than spectacular as compared with its competitors. The fund was in the third quartile for most of this period, and in one case, it was in the fourth quartile.

Why does this happen? There are several common-sense explanations for this phenomenon: (1) Just as the economy moves in cycles, so do asset classes and investment styles. The Vanguard Index 500 Fund is a mirror of the Standard and Poor's 500 Index. It is a large-cap domestic stock index. During some periods, large cap is out of favor compared with other asset classes or investment styles. I plan to visit this question in detail when I cover manager style analysis. (2) In the late 1970s and early 1980s, index investing did not have the cachet with individual investors that it has today. Figure 5–2 shows that the assets under management were not visible on the radar screen in those early days. The demand was simply not there.

Now look at Figure 5–4. This shows the Vanguard Index 500 ranked with its peers, U.S. Large-Cap Funds. The 15-year record excludes the lackluster performance by the Vanguard Index 500 in the late 1970s through early 1980s. It is fair to say that the investor who bought this fund 15 years ago is a happy camper today.

That is great, but what about the next 15 years? Will Large-Cap stocks sink beneath the waves going forward? Will they take a nap for the next 15 years? Of course, nobody knows the answer to that question. I think that a reasonable person can assume that, over the next 15-year period, Large-Cap stocks should at least achieve the long-term average of 9 to 10 percent annual return.

FIGURE 5–4

Vanguard Index 500: Rank with Large-Cap Peers

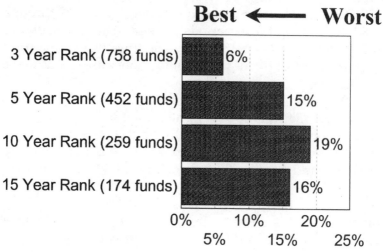

Data Source: Morningstar Principia.

WHAT IS PASSIVE INVESTING?

ACADEMIC POSITION

Market Is a Random Walk   Perhaps the most influential book about passive investing is *A Random Walk Down Wall Street* by Burton Malkiel.[1] Any serious investor should read it. Malkiel, a professor of economics at Princeton University, says that the collective judgment of a competitive market is accurate enough to make individual analysis pointless.

---

1. Burton C. Malkiel, *A Random Walk Down Wall Street* (New York: W.W. Norton, 1973).

Thus, according to Malkiel, the market reflects fair value at all times. We have the framework for a great paradox: Analysis makes the market efficient, but analysis is worthless in an efficient market.

Performance Persistence Is Improbable   A recent contribution to the active-passive debate is a paper by Kahn and Rudd.[2] They are with the economic research and consulting company BARRA that I mentioned in Chapter 3. They tested the popular notion that the best place to look for future mutual fund winners is from a list of past winners. Their work shows *no evidence* of performance persistence for equity mutual funds. They did find limited evidence for persistence of fixed-income funds.

INDUSTRY VIEW

The key players on the other side of this debate come from the major Wall Street firms, from regional brokerage firms, from private money managers, and from active managers in the mutual fund industry. The arguments go something like this: (1) If you are willing to settle for mediocrity, use index funds. Index funds are the market. You cannot expect to do better. (2) Index funds are riskier than actively managed funds. That is so because index funds stay fully invested at all times. Active managers, they argue, have the flexibility to place part of their assets in cash. The theory is that going to higher-than-normal levels of cash can dampen downturns in the market. This cash is then available to cap-

---

2. Ronald N. Kahn and Andrew Rudd, "Does Historical Performance Predict Future Performance?" *Financial Analysts Journal,* November–December 1996, pp. 43–52.

italize on buying opportunities at market lows. (3) If you think about it, the phrase *passive management* even sounds like an oxymoron.

There are other reasons that industry players oppose passive management and index funds. (1) The premise of the industry is that active management can add value over indexing. The premise is inbred into the culture. (2) They have an infrastructure and incentives to support this premise. (3) Promotion of the premise means industry and job security. (4) There are giant egos involved here. (5) It is about fee income. The fees paid for active management are substantially higher (typically by a factor of 2 to 3) than that paid for indexing.

END-USER VIEW

There are end-user groups in this debate. One group consists of the investment committees of major institutional investors. They make use of private money managers. They have a hard time justifying the higher fees of active managers when most do not beat the market.

My experience shows that individual investors have another subjective but practical force at work in favor of actively managed funds. Investing in index funds is, for want of a better word, *dull*. "Index funds take all the fun out of it" are sentiments I hear frequently. The number of index fund offerings out there reflects this lack of demand for index funds beyond the large-cap asset class. As I write this, there are 8,070 funds listed in the Morningstar Principia database. Only 127, or about $1\frac{1}{2}$ percent, of these are in the index category. Many people simply enjoy the thrill of the chase. It is somehow the American way to take risks and to try for the brass ring. Investing becomes as much entertainment and sport as it is a source of wealth for personal goals.

CAN INDEXING MEAN LOWER COSTS?

LOWER EXPENSE RATIOS

Look at Figure 5–5. This shows the expense ratio for the Vanguard Index 500. Calculation of expense ratios puts the internal fund expenses in the numerator and the share price in the denominator. It is the percentage of fund assets paid for operating expenses and management fees including 12b-1 fees, administrative fees, and all other asset-based costs incurred by the fund, except brokerage costs. Fund expenses in this ratio go to the bottom line. They come out of the pocket of the shareholder. Expense ratios do not include sales charges or load fees.

What is a 12b-1 fee? It is an annual charge deducted from fund assets to pay for distribution and marketing costs. Brokers that sell funds with 12b-1 fees receive a commission that is based on the amount of money the investor puts into the fund, and the fee continues as long as the money remains in the fund.

The maximum 12b-1 fee currently allowed by the National Association of Securities Dealers (NASD) is 1 percent or 100 basis points. This can include 25 basis points as "service fees." Brokers get service fees as compensation for continuing contact with clients.

Most private clients I speak with have little or no awareness of mutual fund expense ratios. After I describe the content and the rationale for the fee, they are not happy campers. Most of my clients have a hard time seeing the justification for a 12b-1 fee.

That is not all. Now and then a few funds close temporarily to new investors. As of March 1997, 65 funds in our sample were in this category. According to Morningstar, 22 of those continue to charge a 12b-1 fee. Think about that for a moment: They charge a 12b-1 fee. At the same time, new

FIGURE 5-5

Vanguard Index 500: Expense Ratio

Vanguard Index **500**
Release Date 06-30-97

	Eq Style	FI Style	Morningstar Category
	Large/Blend	-	Large Blend

Performance: History

Expense Ratio

	Current Expense Ratio %	Current 12b-1 Fee	Average Historical Expense Ratio %
● Vanguard Index 500	0.20	0.00	0.28
▨ Large Blend	1.27	0.00	1.27

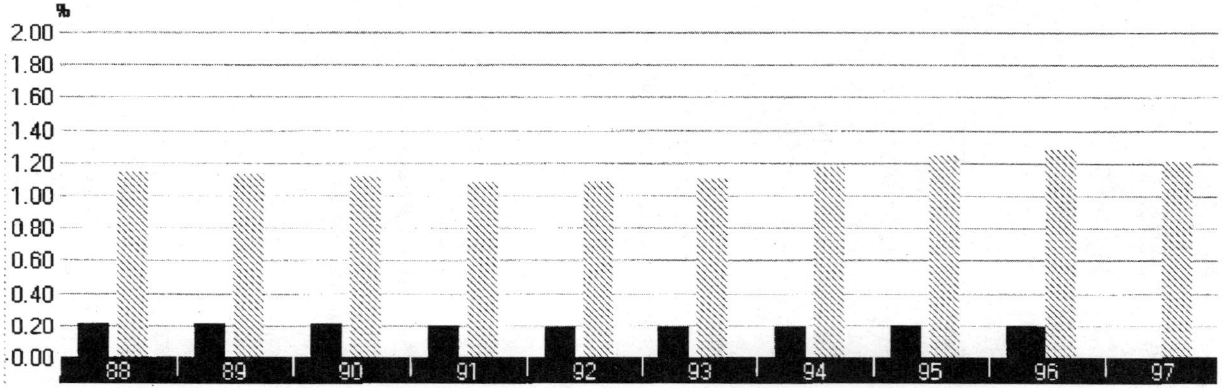

%

2.00
1.80
1.60
1.40
1.20
1.00
0.80
0.60
0.40
0.20
0.00

88 89 90 91 92 93 94 95 96 97

Source: Morningstar Principia.

investors cannot buy the fund! Make your blood boil? I should say!

Should the shareholder care about expense ratios and loads? Look at Figure 5–6. Here I screened for U.S. Equity Diversified Funds. I subdivided these between load and no-load. The load funds have an expense ratio of 1.49 versus 1.04 percent for no-load funds. The 12b-1 fee, as a subset of the expense ratio, is 0.56 percent for load funds and 0.08 percent for no-load funds. According to Morningstar, the 10-year load-adjusted total return is 8.49 percent for load

F I G U R E 5–6

Load Versus No-Load Funds: U.S. Diversified Equity Funds

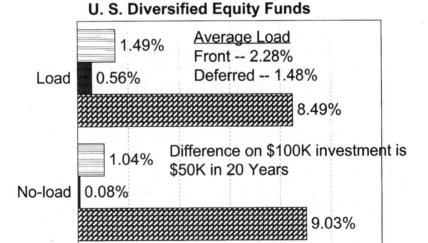

Data Source: Morningstar Principia.

funds and 9.03 percent for no-load funds. The higher expense ratios for load funds appear to be a major cause of the 0.54 percent difference in returns.

That may not seem like a big deal on the surface, but consider this. Assume that a hypothetical client invested $100,000 in a fund paying 8.49 percent and a second $100,000 in a fund paying 9.03 percent. After 20 years, the difference in the balances of the two accounts is over $50,000! I want it to be clear that I am *not* on a crusade to knock load funds or people who sell them. A load fund compensates a broker or a commission-based financial planner for providing advice to the client. It is one valid way to receive compensation. For that, the client should expect competence, objectivity, and quality service on an ongoing basis. I *am* on a crusade to knock funds with excessive expense ratios.

Most investors have familiarity with funds designed and priced for retail distribution. There is another way to deliver mutual funds to investors. The category is *institutional funds*. These are funds designed for purchase by or through institutional investors. Institutional investors, as used here, include registered investment advisors or those purchasing as a fiduciary. In this context, the fund views the end user to be the institutional investor. The institutional investor typically handles the day-to-day interaction with the custodian of the fund. They typically direct purchases and sales of funds on behalf of their client. Institutional funds typically have lower expense ratios than do retail funds. Much of that cost difference comes from the elimination of 12b-1 fees.

As I write this, roughly 15 percent of the funds out there are of the institutional variety. Some are index funds, and some are actively managed. Look at Figure 5–7. It shows a breakout of U.S. Equity, actively managed funds by

FIGURE 5-7

Institutional Versus Retail: U.S. Diversified Equity Funds

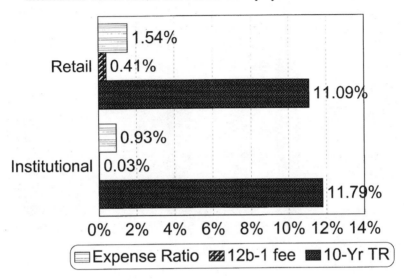

Data Source: Morningstar Principia.

retail and institutional types. The 10-year return for institutional funds is higher that their retail brethren. The difference in 12b-1 fees is the most probable contributor to this higher return.

Look at Figure 5–8. Here I separated U.S. Equity Funds that have an expense ratio history and have at least $10MM in assets. I then ranked them by quartile by expense ratio. Figure 5–8 shows the resulting annualized total return for each group. Remember that total returns shown here include the impact of expense ratios. Notice the gap in return between the group with the lowest expenses and the one with the highest expenses. For a 3-year history, it is

FIGURE 5–8

U.S. Diversified Equity Funds, GE $10MM: Grouped by Expense Ratio

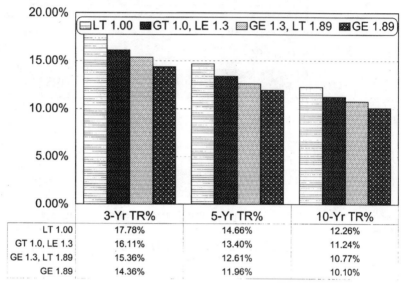

	3-Yr TR%	5-Yr TR%	10-Yr TR%
LT 1.00	17.78%	14.66%	12.26%
GT 1.0, LE 1.3	16.11%	13.40%	11.24%
GE 1.3, LT 1.89	15.36%	12.61%	10.77%
GE 1.89	14.36%	11.96%	10.10%

Data Source: Morningstar Principia.

18.24 − 13.40 = 4.84 percent, or 484 basis points! For a 5-year history, it is 14.75 − 10.31 = 4.44 percent. For a 10-year history, it is 12.25 − 7.85 = 4.40 percent![3]

---

3. A word of caution is in order here. All studies of mutual funds I know about (including the ones you see in this book) suffer from what researchers call *survivorship bias*. What does that mean in plain English? Instead of a statistical analysis, I will put it in terms of the result. Perhaps you have an acquaintance with the field of anthropology. One of the great thinkers in this field was Charles Darwin. He put forth the theory of natural selection, or survival of the fittest. The phrase commonly applied to this theory is "Darwin's law." You may find it helpful to think about survivorship bias as Darwin's law applied to data. In this specific case, the subject is

Let us consider the impact of this on a client. Let us say that your client has an account currently valued at $1 million. One million dollars invested for 20 years at 7.85 percent is $4.5 million. One million dollars invested for 20 years at 12.25 percent is $10.1 million. Now is your blood boiling? Do expense ratios matter? I think so. Advisors and investors should take the time to understand Figure 5–8. Then they should act on what it has to say. Vote with your feet. High expense ratios detract from shareholder return.

There is more. Logic says that, as a fund gets big, the expense ratios should go down. There should be economies of scale passed on to the shareholder. Indeed, Figure 5–9 shows this is the case. Larger funds, on average, have lower expense ratios. The large quartile group has an average size of $263.5MM and an average expense ratio of 1.17 percent. There is a problem here. You cannot automatically assume that a big fund has low expense ratios. As I write this, there are 215 U.S. diversified equity funds in the database with both size and expense ratios that exceed these figures. These funds require further inquiry about expenses before purchase.

Take the popular Kaufmann Fund as an example. This no-load fund attracted almost $5 billion in assets. It has an expense ratio of 2.17 percent. Wait a minute—what is going

---

3. (*Cont.*) mutual fund data. A fund can permanently close or merge. The record disappears, like magic, from the radar screen. If the demand for a fund is not there, the fund company simply takes it off the shelf. I do not suggest here that this is wrong or improper. After all, not every product that a company manufactures is a smashing success. Sometimes it is better to cut your losses and move on. *Survivorship bias* is a term often used by study critics. They appropriately point out that the data reflect statistics only on the funds that remain standing at any point in the battle. That is your 2-minute workout on survivorship bias.

FIGURE 5–9

Expense Ratios, U.S. Diversified Equity Funds:
Grouped by Asset Size, $MM

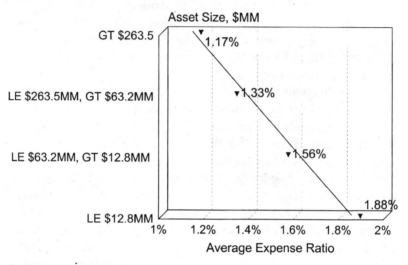

Data Source: Morningstar Principia.

on here? When you lift the hood, you find that there is a management fee of 150 basis points and a 12b-1 fee of 75 basis points![4]

Here is a little exercise to keep you awake. Compute the management fee paid to Kaufmann. Take 1.5 percent of $4,857,200,000 in assets. Not a bad day's pay! Fortunately for the portfolio managers, Lawrence Auriana and Hans Utsch, there is a good performance record that keeps them near the front of the pack in spite of their hefty expense

---

4. *Source:* Morningstar Principia.

ratio. Even so, there are 5 funds in their peer group with a better record and a lower expense ratio. I looked at the 10 other top-ranked small-company growth funds with at least a 5-year record. The average management fee is 81 basis points, and the average 12b-1 fee is 15 basis points. The average fund size of the other 10 funds is $872MM— about one-fifth the size of Kaufmann. Why is Kaufmann so much larger? Of course, they have a great record. However, could the extra money from 12b-1 fees poured into marketing and distribution be another reason? Remember that shareholders pay the 12b-1 fee!

LOWER TRANSACTION COSTS

There are other costs not included in the expense ratio. Look at Figure 5–10. This shows the turnover of the portfolio for the Vanguard Index 500. Remember that the index reflects decisions by the folks at Standard and Poor's about the content of the index. They generally pick Large Cap stocks with strong financial statements and industry leadership. Therefore, the Vanguard Index 500 as well as other index funds based on the S&P 500 Index are *actively managed,* figuratively speaking, by Standard & Poor's.

The turnover activity is quite small compared with the typical equity mutual fund. Lately it has been roughly 5 percent. A 5 percent turnover translates into a 20-year holding period on average. That means fewer transaction costs passed on to the shareholder compared with high-turnover funds. Transaction costs include brokerage cost and the spread between the bid and ask price of the security bought or sold. A reasonable estimate of brokerage costs is 50 to 60 basis points. Bid-ask spreads can exceed 500 basis points for very small stocks.

F I G U R E 5–10

Vanguard Index 500: Portfolio Turnover

Vanguard Index 500
Release Date: 03-31-97

EQ Style ⊞ Large/Blend

FI Style -

Objective Growth and Income

Performance: History

Current Turnover Rate -

Average Historical Turnover Rate 847

Turnover
● Vanguard Index 500

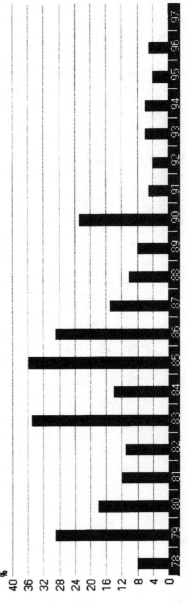

Source: Morningstar Principia.

POTENTIAL FOR LOWER TAX COST

High turnover *may* also mean high tax costs. While this has no significance for a qualified retirement plan or an IRA, it does affect a taxable portfolio. A few active fund managers out there systematically attempt to match capital losses with gains to minimize the tax impact. Many active managers that I speak with do not pay attention to tax management. A screen of Morningstar Principia shows only 18 funds as of March 1997 that represent that they focus on tax management. I spoke with other managers about this. Only a few do it. Some say they look at tax implications in the fourth quarter of each year. On behalf of all taxable investors out there, I would like to appeal to active managers to focus on this matter. It is another way to set yourself apart from the pack.

Some critics of index funds say that the low turnover of index funds produces substantially higher capital gains overhang than that of actively managed funds. This argument does not hold up under scrutiny. Let us look at the facts. Capital gain overhang is a risk that investors face. It represents *unrealized* capital gain. It measures the degree to which assets of a fund have the potential to trigger tax on liquidation. Figure 5–11 shows that the median for index funds is 23 percent and the median for active U.S. Diversified Equity Funds is 19 percent. Figure 5–12 shows the same information for Large Cap U.S. Diversified Equity Funds. The median here is 23 percent for index funds and 21 percent for active funds. There is not much of a gap here.

Next, look at Figure 5–13. It shows the range of turnover of assets with a fund. It compares Large Cap U.S. Diversified Equity Index Funds with active funds. Note the median turnover of 8 percent for index funds and 60 per-

FIGURE 5–11

Capital Gain Overhang: U.S. Diversified Equity Funds

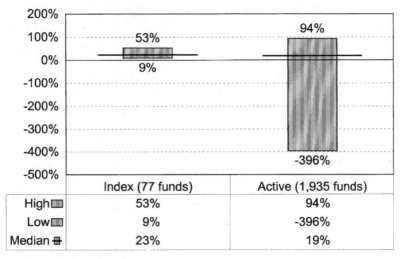

	Index (77 funds)	Active (1,935 funds)
High▥	53%	94%
Low▥	9%	-396%
Median ⊟	23%	19%

Data Source: Morningstar Principia.

cent for active funds. That is a ratio of 7 to 1. A reasonable person can conclude from these data that the greater risk of *realizing* capital gain overhang lies with active funds. This is not from market downturns that drive up fund redemptions; rather, it happens as a result of day-to-day management with an average turnover of 60 percent.

Should the shareholder care about turnover? Look at Figure 5–14. This is similar to Figure 5–8 except I grouped the funds into quartiles ranked by turnover. Figure 5–8 showed an inverse relationship between expense ratio and total return. Figure 5–14 shows a similar relationship between turnover and total return. The spread between the

F I G U R E 5–12

Capital Gain Overhang: Large Cap U.S. Diversified Funds,
Index Versus Active

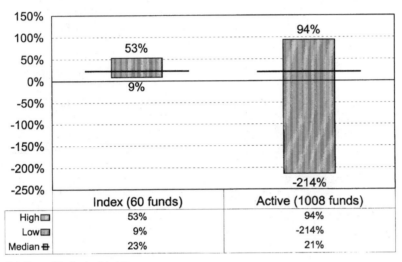

	Index (60 funds)	Active (1008 funds)
High	53%	94%
Low	9%	-214%
Median	23%	21%

Data Source: Morningstar Principia.

top and bottom group for a 10-year period is 1.46 percent,
or 146 basis points. This is not quite as dramatic as Figure
5–8. Even so, it is worth our attention. The shareholder need
not leave this money on the table.

LITTLE OR NO SALES CHARGE

With a few exceptions, index funds have no front-end or
deferred sales charges. As I write this, there are 127 index
funds shown in the Morningstar database. Of those, 16 have
front-end loads, and 6 have deferred loads. The rest (83 per-

FIGURE 5-13

Turnover: Large Cap U.S. Diversified Equity, Index Versus Active

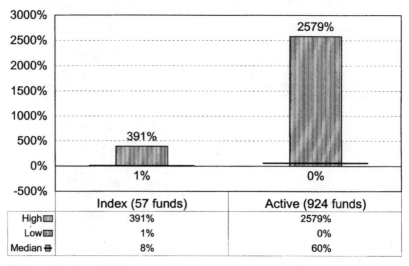

	Index (57 funds)	Active (924 funds)
High	391%	2579%
Low	1%	0%
Median	8%	60%

Data Source: Morningstar Principia.

cent of the total) are no-load. I often wonder how folks running an index fund can justify a sales load. Think about that
one! We have the ingredients here for yet another oxymoron. Caveat emptor!

FIGURE 5–14

U.S. Diversified Equity Funds: Grouped by Turnover

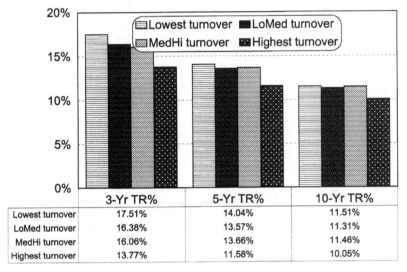

	3-Yr TR%	5-Yr TR%	10-Yr TR%
Lowest turnover	17.51%	14.04%	11.51%
LoMed turnover	16.38%	13.57%	11.31%
MedHi turnover	16.06%	13.66%	11.46%
Highest turnover	13.77%	11.58%	10.05%

Data Source: Morningstar Principia.

Index Funds—What Is Out There

INDEX FUNDS AVAILABLE NOW

An index fund should produce the same return and risk characteristics as the underlying index after adjustment for expenses. There were 127 index funds out there as of March 1997.[1] Think about it: There are 6,000 to 8,000 mutual funds, depending on how you count share categories. Let us use 6,000 for this illustration. Out of that, only 2 percent are index funds. This is hardly a ringing endorsement. Many index funds (35 of 127) have been in existence for only 3 years or less.

Refer to Figure 6–1. Large Cap Stock Funds dominate the pie chart. This makes sense: (1) It is the closest to the ideal of an efficient market. There are hundreds of analysts sifting every crumb of data, weighing every rumor about companies in this asset class. Some investors know this and

---

1. *Source:* Morningstar Principia.

127 Index Funds by Category

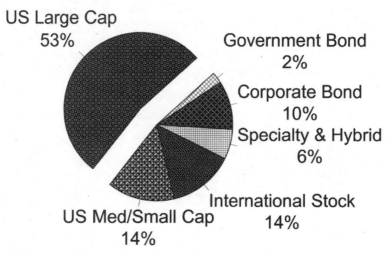

US Large Cap 53%

Government Bond 2%

Corporate Bond 10%

Specialty & Hybrid 6%

International Stock 14%

US Med/Small Cap 14%

Data Source: Morningstar Principia.

conclude that active management is a waste of time here. (2) Fund companies want a piece of the action they see at the Vanguard Index 500. There is something like a feeding frenzy happening. Other categories are following. These new categories of index funds reflect a demand for asset class investing.

Refer next to Figure 6–2. This shows the categories of index funds together with statistical averages of expense ratios and turnover for each category. This makes it clear that you cannot take just any index fund and get low cost and low turnover.

Earlier, I discussed a claim made by the index opponents. The opponents say that index funds carry more risk than active funds because index funds stay fully invested. They say that active managers have the flexibility to go to

FIGURE 6–2

127 Index Funds: Expense Ratio and Turnover

	Expense Ratio, %	Turnover, %
US Large Cap	0.56	18
US Med/Small Cap	0.81	32
International Stock	0.98	15
Specialty/Hybrid	0.65	23
Corporate Bond	0.4	94
Government Bond	0.3	50

Data Source: Morningstar Principia.

cash in overvalued markets. Look at Figure 6–3. This shows the Morningstar risk (downside risk) for U.S. Diversified Equity Funds for 3-, 5-, and 10-year periods. There is a sep-

FIGURE 6–3

Downside Risk: Index Versus Actively Managed,
U.S. Diversified Equity Funds

Type	3-Yr MS Risk	5-Yr MS Risk	10 Yr MS Risk
Index (85 funds)	0.82	0.85	1.02
Active (2,248 funds)	1.09	1.06	1.04

Data Source: Morningstar Principia.

aration into two groups. The first group is index funds; the second group is actively managed funds. These data refute that claim. The downside risk for all three periods is less for index funds than it is for active funds.

A NEW BREED?

The word is out. There is a new fund subcategory in town. Morningstar refers to them as "enhanced index funds." Like an index fund, this group attempts to match an index performance. Unlike an index fund, they attempt to better the index. One way is by adding value through selective stock picking. Another is by reducing volatility with derivatives. There are 49 of them as I write this.[2] Only 20 have 3 or more years of accomplishment. Many of them use quantitative analysis.

Are these index funds or actively managed funds? Let us consult with our old friend the duck: If it looks like, walks like, and quacks like a duck, it must be a duck. Check Figure 6–4. If you consider expense ratio and turnover, they seem more like active funds. If you consider downside risk, they seem more like index funds. Are they index or active? The answer is yes.

A LIVE EXAMPLE OF PASSIVE INVESTING

Want to visit a living laboratory focused on buy-and-hold, passive investing? Here is a classic. It is the Lexington Corporate Leaders Fund. Let us stop by and kick the tires. The inception date is November 1935. The charter specified

---

2. *Source:* Morningstar Principia.

FIGURE 6–4

Index Funds: Classic Versus Enhanced

Type	Expense Ratio	Turnover	3-Yr MS Risk
Enhanced (49 funds)	1.11%	84%	0.82
Classic (127 funds)	0.64%	30%	0.89
Active (2,248 funds)	1.46%	90%	1.09

Data Source: Morningstar Principia.

the purchase of 30 stocks thought to have good long-term potential for growth. The manager cannot buy new names. He can sell stocks but only those that no longer pay dividends or fit the corporate leader criteria. Twenty-three of the original holdings remain in the portfolio today. There were spin-offs over the years that appear in the portfolio. The expense ratio of this fund is 0.63 percent today. Turnover is a moot point. Cast your eyes on Figure 6–5. Look at the 20-year record of this fund. It beat the S&P by 8 basis points. It ranks in the top 4 percent within its category. There is no 12b-1 fee here. What a great story!

GOT THE WRONG IMPRESSION?

On a lighter note, consider the following. When I entered this business, I was young and impressionable—okay, impressionable. I thought of the Vanguard Group and

Buy-and-Hold, Passive Investing: Lexington Corporate Leaders

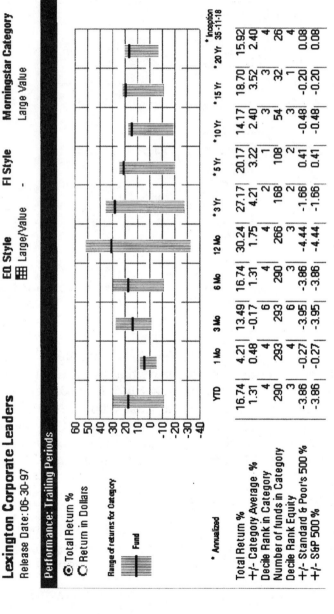

Lexington Corporate Leaders
Release Date: 06-30-97

EQ Style	FI Style	Morningstar Category
▦ Large/Value	-	Large Value

Performance: Trailing Periods

◯ Total Return %
◯ Return in Dollars

Range of returns for Category

Fund

* Annualized

	YTD	1 Mo	3 Mo	6 Mo	12 Mo	*3 Yr	*5 Yr	*10 Yr	*15 Yr	*20 Yr	*Inception 35-11-18
Total Return %	16.74	4.21	13.49	16.74	30.24	27.17	20.17	14.17	18.70	15.92	-
+/- Category Average %	1.31	0.48	-0.17	1.31	1.75	4.21	3.22	2.40	3.52	2.40	-
Decile Rank in Category	4	4	6	4	4	2	1	3	3	4	-
Number of funds in Category	290	293	293	290	266	168	108	54	32	26	-
Decile Rank Equity	3	4	6	3	3	2	2	3	1	4	-
+/- Standard & Poor's 500 %	-3.86	-0.27	-3.95	-3.86	-4.44	-1.66	0.41	-0.48	-0.20	0.08	-
+/- S&P 500 %	-3.86	-0.27	-3.95	-3.86	-4.44	-1.66	0.41	-0.48	-0.20	0.08	-

Source: Morningstar Principia.

Dimensional Fund Advisors (DFA) as the leaders of the charge toward passive investing and indexing. My perception of these two firms was that they represented the random walk in action. I suppose that this is mainly due to the speeches (read that as *sermons*) I heard by John Bogle of Vanguard and Rex Sinquefield of DFA. I felt that I was in the presence of someone that would seek the higher ground and take the road less traveled as expressed by Frost.[3] Perhaps you felt the same way.

Au contraire! When I arrived at the party, I got a surprise. As I write this, Vanguard has 76 funds in the Morningstar database, but only 17 of them have an "index" on their name tag. DFA has 24 funds there, but only 8 of them have an "index" name tag. What is going on here? Did I come to the wrong party? Is it the right address but the wrong date? Are the folks at Morningstar confused? Can it be true that Vanguard and DFA both have more nonindex funds than index funds? What exactly are these nonindex funds? Could they be, dare I say it, actively managed? Exit stage left idealism. Enter stage right pragmatism and the drive for market share. Nothing personal, just business.

CONCLUSION

Figures 5–8 and 5–14 send a strong message to advisors, to investors, and to fund companies. It is not about indexing—it is about cost. Proxies for cost are expense ratio, turnover, and capital gain overhang. High cost

> It is not about indexing—it is about cost. The level of fund costs reflects the attitude of management.

---

3. Robert Frost, *Choice*.

can severely impair the record of an otherwise good active manager. Turnover is controllable by the manger.

The level of fund costs reflects the attitude of management. The fund executives and the manager should realize that high costs adversely affect the performance record and, thus, demand for the fund. They should be sensitive to this fact and take appropriate action. If they fail to act, the shareholders should act. Shareholders do not have to take it anymore!

Here is the other side of this discussion. Indexing does not automatically give you low cost. As of March 1997, there were eight index funds in the Morningstar database with expense ratios of 1.50 percent or greater. The highest is 2.50 percent. There are four index funds with a turnover greater than 100 percent. One has a turnover approaching 400 percent! Here is a warning. Read the label before you buy!

We should broaden our consideration of this topic to include the general meaning of *passive investing*. I like to think of passive investing as mostly a buy-and-hold, long-term strategy. The grouping can include actively managed funds with low expense ratios and low turnover. When we do this, it expands our range of choice by a considerable margin. In this context, index funds become only one avenue for implementation of the long-term, passive-investing concept.

The expense ratio breakpoint for the best quartile in Figure 5–8 is 0.98 percent. The turnover breakpoint for the best quartile in Figure 5–14 is 36 percent. If I screen the Morningstar database for U.S. Diversified Equity Funds that are not index funds but have an expense ratio less than 0.98 percent, I find 429 funds. If I add a turnover of less than 36 percent, I still find 112 funds.

My feeling is that buy-and-hold, a.k.a. passive invest-ing, is a viable strategy for a private client. Passive invest-ing suggests low cost. It is long-term in time horizon. Index funds can be a part of that strategy. They must, however, compete with other low-cost actively managed funds. A dogmatic approach calling for exclusive use of index funds is not, in my judgment, in the best interests of the Private Client.

CHAPTER 7

Active Investing

PROLOGUE

This chapter is about selection of active mutual fund managers. Assembling a portfolio of active managers that meets or exceeds an index approach is time-consuming and difficult. Some say impossible. People who think they can do a thorough job of due diligence with a few computer searches and star rankings are naive and mistaken. An advisor with an attitude like that becomes part of the problem, not the solution. Advisors should approach the due diligence investigation of active mutual fund managers with the same level of care and attention to detail as they would private placements and direct investments.

People who think they can do a thorough job of due diligence with a few computer searches and star rankings are naive and mistaken.

Let me use a metaphor from the legal profession. A

prosecuting attorney or a defense attorney accumulates as much evidence as possible to prove his or her case. First, there is direct evidence such as eyewitness testimony. Second, there is indirect or circumstantial evidence such as fingerprints. The goal of the attorney is to find as much corroborating direct and circumstantial evidence as possible to make a convincing case.

Successful selection of active managers also requires gathering as much direct and indirect evidence as possible. The advisor must consider *all* evidence. It must be the weight of the evidence, both good and bad, that supports the up or down decision.

After the selection of active managers, the process continues. The advisor must constantly monitor what the fund manager does. Consider this analogy. You board a cruise ship in Vancouver that you believe is bound for Alaska. That evening, the ship gets underway. The next morning you wake up to find that your ship is off the coast of California headed for the Panama Canal. Active managers can and do change their strategy and style. Active managers move to other funds, forcing the fund company to find a new manager.

If you want to have a voice about the course and destination of the portfolio of your client, you must stay engaged. You must have the information to make an informed decision at any point before or during the journey. That means that you must make periodic visits to the bridge to read the vital signs of not only the ship but also the captain. You can hire someone to do part of this data gathering for you, but it must be someone or a firm that you have confidence in. Make no mistake: The buck stops with you. The client looks to you the advisor, not the mutual fund reporting service, for leadership and sound advice.

WORLD-CLASS ACTIVE INVESTORS

This chapter is for those who believe that there are ineffi-
ciencies in the securities markets. You believe that there are
always opportunities to find bargains. I begin by paying my
respects to those who did it. Who are the great active
investors, and what can we learn from them?

WARREN BUFFETT

Warren Buffett is the captain of the ship at Berkshire
Hathaway. Depending on how and when you count, he is
either number 1 or 2 in wealth in this country. His basic
approach to investing is from the value school of Benjamin
Graham. Buffett puts his own stamp on his strategy with an
added focus on companies with strong franchises and high
quality and sustainability of earnings. He buys businesses
in low-tech industries that are easily understood. The vice
chairman of Berkshire is Charles Munger. He helps Buffett
to set the strategy and to select the investments made by the
company.

To own Berkshire Hathaway is much like owning a
great mutual fund. The core business of Berkshire Hathaway
is insurance underwriting including the acquisition of
GEICO. In addition, they own substantial interests in fran-
chise brand names like Coca-Cola, Gillette, American
Express Co., Wells Fargo & Company, The Walt Disney
Company, Federal Home Loan Mortgage Corp., McDonald's
Corp., and The Washington Post Co. They also acquired out-
right Dexter Shoes, Sees Candies, Scott & Fetzer, Helzberg's
Diamond Shops, Inc., R.C. Willey Home Furnishings, and
H.H. Brown Shoe Co.

Cast your eyes on Figure 7–1. This shows the growth
of $1 million invested in Berkshire Hathaway in March

Warren Buffett: World-Class Investor, Berkshire Hathaway Stock
Growth of $1 Million Investment

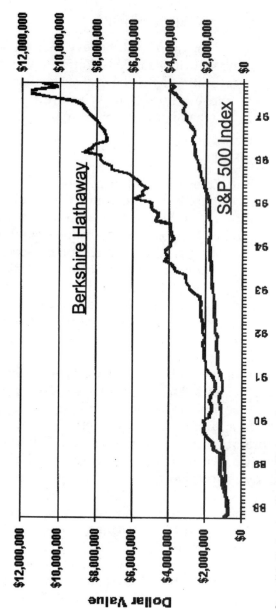

Source: ValueLine Investment Survey for Windows.

1987. Ten years later the worth of this hypothetical portfolio is $10.2 million. That is an annual growth rate of better than 26 percent compounded. In the same period the S&P grew by roughly 13 percent compounded.

Not everyone can afford to own the voting A shares of the company. As I write this, the price per share is in the range of $38,000. Those who sit and wait for a stock split may wish to bring along a good novel or two to read.

Two mutual funds have sizeable holdings in Berkshire. One is the Sequoia Fund, which has been managed by William Ruane and Richard Cunniff since 1970. They have a 20-year annual return of 19 percent. That is 364 basis points better than the S&P 500. Berkshire Hathaway shares make up roughly 27 percent of the value of the portfolio. Sequoia also holds two names held by Buffett: Federal Home Loan Mortgage Corp. and Walt Disney. Adding these two stocks makes the Buffett-like portion of the portfolio 44 percent of the total. The total of names held by the fund is currently 15. Unfortunately, the fund closed to new investors in 1982.[1] In spite of this, Morningstar continues to provide a periodic analysis of this fund. That should give you some idea of their respect for these two managers. If your aging relative or friend holds a few Sequoia shares, ask them to remember you in their will. It seems that is the only way to get in at this point.

The next in line to provide a Buffett-like presence is the Focus Fund managed by Robert Hagstrom. This fund opened its doors in April 1995. It has less than $10 million in assets as I write this. Hagstrom holds 16 names. Berkshire

---

1. Funds closed to new investors may be still available through your advisor or through an investor matchmaking service provided by Jack White & Co. Unfortunately, Sequoia is not one of these.

Hathaway makes up roughly 8 percent of the portfolio. He also holds some of the same names owned by Berkshire Hathaway, that is, American Express, Walt Disney, Federal Home Loan Mortgage, and Washington Post Class B. The total of the portfolio that is Berkshire or Berskshire holdings is roughly 35 percent. The remainder of the names represents a Buffett-like strategy. You can tell that Hagstrom follows the Buffett playbook. It appears not only in the names he chooses but also in his selection process and the willingness to concentrate his choices.

The Berkshire Hathaway annual shareholder meetings are as entertaining as they are informative. At a recent meeting, Munger referred to Modern Portfolio Theory as "twaddle." This word, I must confess, is not part of my everyday vocabulary. For those of you who are afraid to ask, it means "silly," "ridiculous," or "absurd." By inference, I suppose those who offer twaddle are twaddlers. Proper usage might be, "Twaddlers often engage in promoting their twaddle." Buffett was equally succinct. He offered an opinion about diversification as a strategy. He said that owning even 30 stocks is "crazy." He said, "Diversification is protection against ignorance. It makes very little sense for those who know what they are doing."[2]

PETER LYNCH

If you did some of your investing during the 1980s, you have probably heard of Peter Lynch. His accomplishments are legendary as manager of the Fidelity Magellan Fund. His tenure there spanned the period from May 1977 through June 1990. Figure 7–2 shows his accomplishments

2. *Barron's Online*, http://www.barrons.com, July 20, 1996.

FIGURE 7-2

Peter Lynch, Tenure at Fidelity Magellan
May 1977–June 1990

Fidelity Magellan
03-31-97

	EQ Style	FI Style	Objective
	Large/Value	-	Growth

Performance: History

Total Return	Time Period	Total Return %	Annualized Total Return %
● Fund Fidelity Magellan	Jan 70 - Mar 97	9048.08	18.03
◐ Primary Index Standard & Poor's F	Jan 70 - Mar 97	-	-
◑● Secondary Index Wilshire Top 75i	Jan 70 - Mar 97		
● Objective Growth	Jan 70 - Mar 97	1869.51	11.56

Total Return %

Indicates data for partial years

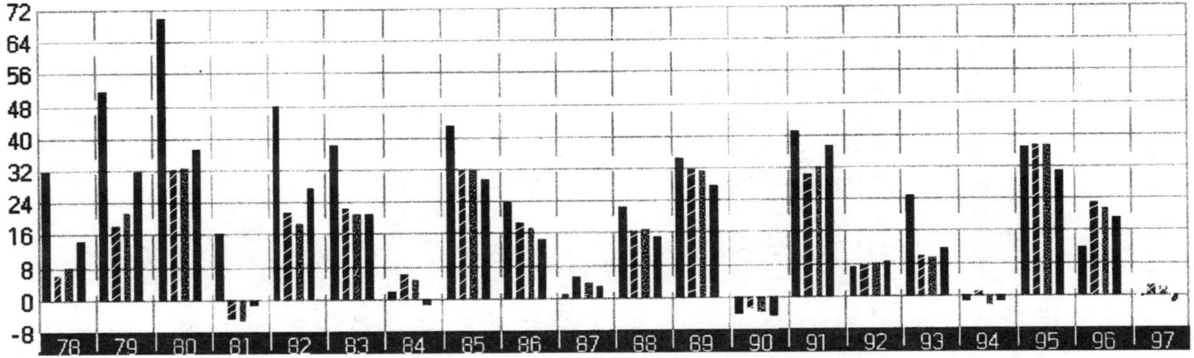

Source: Morningstar Principia.

from 1978 until 1990. For each year, the vertical bar on the far left is the record of the fund.

Lynch practiced growth investing. It was earnings growth but at a reasonable price. Some people call it *growth at a reasonable price,* or GARP. Like Buffett, he advocates investing in businesses that you can understand.

I do not have figures about Lynch's personal wealth. Nevertheless, walk with me through a hypothetical exercise. Let us suppose that Lynch wanted to accumulate additional personal wealth starting in 1977. Let us say that he put $1 million into his fund on the day he took over. Then he held his shares including reinvested distributions through his resignation as manager. At the end of his tenure at Magellan, the terminal value of his account would be $27.5 million! That is a 24.4 percent compounded annual return! Figure 7–3 shows this. Fund reporting services typically list performance on a before-tax basis in this way. Figure 7–4 shows the same facts except with an investment in the Vanguard Index 500. The terminal value of the account would be $6.2 million.

Now let us be even more conservative. Let us assume this was a taxable account and that he sold shares to pay taxes on distributions over the years. At the end of his tenure, he would have $18.7 million in the account. Unrealized capital gain would be $10.9 million. Let us say that he then liquidated shares and paid the capital gains tax. That would leave him with $15.7 million free and clear. You can see this in Figure 7–5. Under this scenario, would he have enough cash to allow him to retire in comfort? I suspect so! Figure 7–6 shows the same facts except with an investment in the Vanguard Index 500. The free and clear terminal cash is $3.8 million.

FIGURE 7-3

Peter Lynch, Hypothetical Account—Before Tax:
Invest $1 Million in Fidelity Magellan, Reinvest Distributions
May 1977–June 1990

Portfolio: FM1

Fidelity Magellan from 05-01-77 to 06-30-90

	Cumulative $
Initial Investment	1,000,000
⠿ Total Net Investment	13,858,580
● Final Market Value	27,506,393
Unrealized Capital Gain/Loss	13,647,813

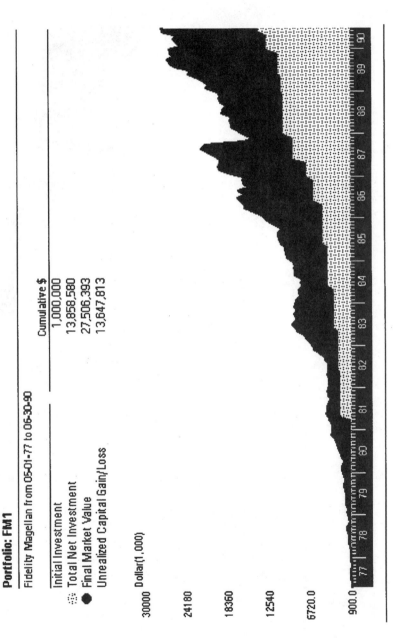

Source: Morningstar Principia.

163

FIGURE 7-4

Peter Lynch, Hypothetical Account—Before Tax:
Invest $1 Million in Vanguard Index 500, Reinvest Distributions
May 1977–June 1990

Portfolio: VG1

Vanguard Index 500 from 05-01-77 to 06-30-90

	Cumulative $
Initial Investment	1,000,000
Total Net Investment	3,349,464
Final Market Value	6,196,493
Unrealized Capital Gain/Loss	2,847,028

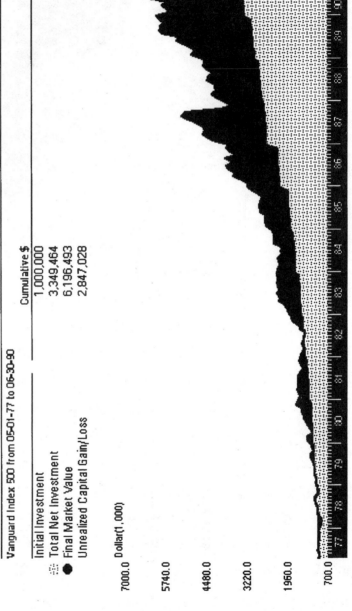

Source: Morningstar Principia.

FIGURE 7-5

Peter Lynch, Hypothetical Account—After Tax:
Invest $1 Million in Fidelity Magellan, Reinvest Distributions—Sell Shares to Pay Tax
May 1977–June 1990

Portfolio: FM1

Fidelity Magellan from 05-01-77 to 06-30-90

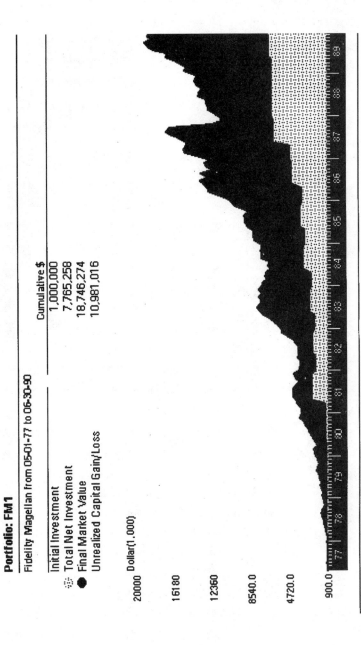

	Cumulative $
Initial Investment	1,000,000
Total Net Investment	7,765,258
Final Market Value	18,746,274
Unrealized Capital Gain/Loss	10,981,016

165

F I G U R E 7-6

Peter Lynch, Hypothetical Account—After Tax:
Invest $1 Million in Vanguard Index 500, Reinvest Distributions—Sell Shares to Pay Tax
May 1977–June 1990

Portfolio: VG1

Vanguard Index 500 from 05-01-77 to 06-30-90

	Cumulative $
Initial Investment	1,000,000
Total Net Investment	2,212,033
Final Market Value	4,484,906
Unrealized Capital Gain/Loss	2,272,874

Dollar(1,000)

Source: Morningstar Principia.

WHY ARE THERE NOT MORE LEGENDARY INVESTORS?

I hear this question often in passive-versus-active debates. The short answer is, they are not easy to find but there are some. They may not be legends, but they are very good, bordering on great. Let us consider a few managers.

TOP MANAGERS WITH A 15-YEAR RECORD OF ACCOMPLISHMENT

Mairs & Power Growth Fund

The manager of this fund is George Mairs III. He has been at the wheel for 17 years. His 20-year record of accomplishment is 15½ percent, or 45 basis points, above the S&P 500 (see Figure 7–7). For the last 15 years the return was 18 percent, or in the top decile of equity funds. The fund is the Large Cap Core Fund. (Morningstar uses the word "Blend" instead of "Core.") The 15-year record is 18 percent. This puts the fund in the top decile for that period.

The 3-year downside risk (Morningstar risk) is 0.80. The Sharpe ratio is an extraordinary 1.86 percent. Like Buffett, Mairs believes in concentration. His top 10 holdings make up 48 percent of his total assets.

The expense ratio is 0.99 percent, and the turnover is only 4 percent. That is a holding period of 25 years.

Washington Mutual Investors

This fund is another exception to one of my rules. I generally look for a strong personality found in a single manager or, at least, lead manager. This fund has *eight* managers. You probably know all the same bad jokes that I do about the value of committees. This one seems to work. The average tenure is 9 years.

For one thing, there are some heavy hitters there. For

FIGURE 7-7

George Mairs III: Mairs & Power Growth Fund

Mairs & Power Growth
Release Date: 06-30-97

EQ Style Medium/Blend
FI Style -
Morningstar Category Mid-Cap Blend

Performance: Trailing Periods

Legend: ● Total Return % ○ Return in Dollars Range of returns for Category Fund

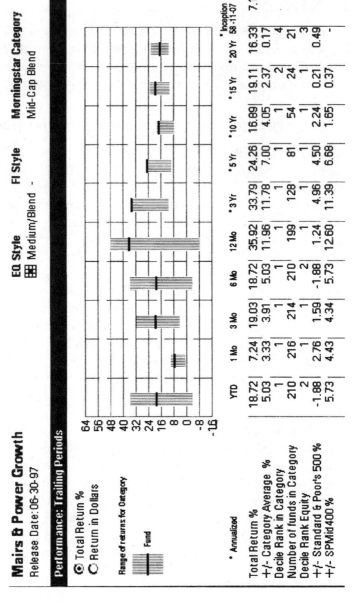

	YTD	1 Mo	3 Mo	6 Mo	12 Mo	3 Yr*	5 Yr*	10 Yr*	15 Yr*	20 Yr*	Inception* 58-11-07
Total Return %	18.72	7.24	19.03	18.72	35.92	33.79	24.26	16.89	19.11	16.33	7.16
+/- Category Average %	5.03	3.33	3.91	5.03	11.96	11.78	7.00	4.05	2.37	0.17	-
Decile Rank in Category	1	1	1	1	1	1	1	1	2	4	-
Number of funds in Category	210	216	214	210	199	128	81	54	24	21	-
Decile Rank Equity	2	1	1	2	1	1	1	1	1	3	-
+/- Standard & Poor's 500 %	-1.88	2.76	1.59	-1.88	1.24	4.96	4.50	2.24	0.21	0.49	-
+/- SPMid400 %	5.73	4.43	4.34	5.73	12.60	11.39	6.68	1.65	0.37	-	-

* Annualized

Source: Morningstar Principia.

instance, James Dunton is a former chair of the Financial Analysts Federation and the present chair of the Association for Investment Management and Research (AIMR). The AIMR, together with the Investment Management Consultants Association (IMCA), provides standards for measurement of investment managers.

Second, they all use the same playbook. The prospectus calls for purchase of stocks that are legal for investment trust funds in the District of Columbia. The idea is to act in a manner consistent with someone having a fiduciary responsibility under the *Prudent Man Rules.* They select only the bluest of blue chips that have consistently increased dividends over the years. This fund is one of 25 that make up the American Funds Group. Another large fund in this group is the Investment Company of America. These funds have a team approach also.

Figure 7–8 shows the record of this team, which has a 20-year record of roughly 16 percent and a 15-year record of about 18 percent. That is 89 and 34 basis points ahead of the S&P 500. The 3-year downside risk of this fund is 0.64. The Sharpe ratio is 1.86. The expense ratio is 0.66 percent, and the turnover is 24 percent.

Enterprise Growth A

The manager of this fund for the last 17 years has been Ronald Canakaris. It is a Large Cap Growth Fund. Figure 7–9 shows his record: 16 percent + for 20 years and 17 percent + for 15 years. That is 114 and 3 basis points, respectively, better than the S&P 500.

The 3-year downside (Morningstar) risk is 1.15. The Sharpe ratio is 1.29. The expense ratio is 1.60, and the turnover is 45 percent. This is a Large Cap Growth Fund. The expense ratio is a drag on performance, but the magnitude of the return still pulls the fund into the top grouping.

FIGURE 7-8

James Dunton et al.: Washington Mutual Investors

Washington Mutual Investors
Release Date: 06-30-97

EQ Style	FI Style	Morningstar Category
⊞ Large/Value	-	Large Value

Performance: Trailing Periods

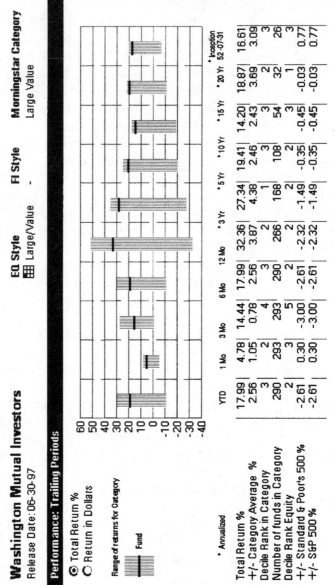

Legend:
- ⊚ Total Return %
- ○ Return in Dollars

Range of returns for Category: Fund

* Annualized	YTD	1 Mo	3 Mo	6 Mo	12 Mo	* 3 Yr	* 5 Yr	* 10 Yr	* 15 Yr	* 20 Yr	* Inception 52-07-31
Total Return %	17.99	4.78	14.44	17.99	32.36	27.34	19.41	14.20	18.87	16.61	--
+/- Category Average %	2.56	1.05	0.78	2.56	3.87	4.38	2.46	2.43	3.69	3.09	--
Decile Rank in Category	3	2	4	3	2	1	3	3	2	3	--
Number of funds in Category	290	293	293	290	266	168	108	54	32	26	--
Decile Rank Equity	2	3	5	2	2	2	2	3	1	3	--
+/- Standard & Poor's 500 %	-2.61	0.30	-3.00	-2.61	-2.32	-1.49	-0.35	-0.45	-0.03	0.77	--
+/- S&P 500 %	-2.61	0.30	-3.00	-2.61	-2.32	-1.49	-0.35	-0.45	-0.03	0.77	--

Source: Morningstar Principia.

FIGURE 7-9

Ronald Canakaris: Enterprise Growth A

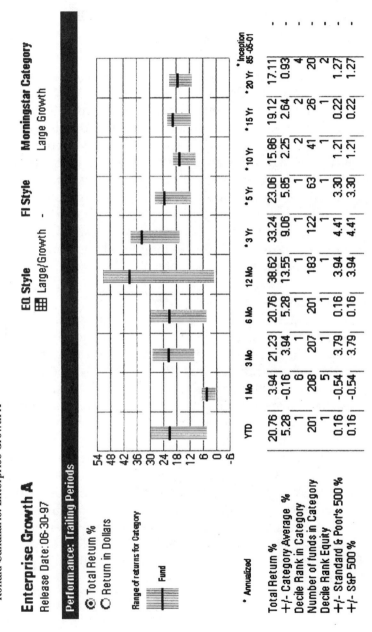

Enterprise Growth A
Release Date: 06-30-97

EQ Style Large/Growth

FI Style -

Morningstar Category Large Growth

Performance: Trailing Periods

Legend:
- Total Return %
- Return in Dollars
- Range of returns for Category
- Fund

	YTD	1 Mo	3 Mo	6 Mo	12 Mo	*3 Yr	*5 Yr	*10 Yr	*15 Yr	*20 Yr	*Inception 85-05-01
Total Return %	20.76	3.94	21.23	20.76	38.62	33.24	23.06	15.86	19.12	17.11	-
+/- Category Average %	5.28	-0.16	3.94	5.28	13.55	9.06	5.85	2.25	2.64	0.93	-
Decile Rank in Category	1	6	1	1	1	1	1	2	2	4	-
Number of funds in Category	201	208	207	201	183	122	63	41	26	20	-
Decile Rank Equity	1	5	1	1	1	1	1	1	1	2	-
+/- Standard & Poor's 500 %	0.16	-0.54	3.79	0.16	3.94	4.41	3.30	1.21	0.22	1.27	-
+/- S&P 500 %	0.16	-0.54	3.79	0.16	3.94	4.41	3.30	1.21	0.22	1.27	-

* Annualized

Source: Morningstar Principia.

TOP FUNDS WITH AT LEAST A 10-YEAR RECORD OF ACCOMPLISHMENT

MAS Value Institutional

The lead manager of the MAS Value Institutional Fund is Robert Marchin. Comanagers are Nicholas Kovich and Richard Behler. The average manager tenure is 4 years. It is a Large Cap Value Fund. The 10-year record is $14\frac{1}{2}$ percent compounded, and the 5-year record is $19\frac{1}{2}$ percent compounded. That is 111 and 310 basis points better than the S&P 500. The record of the fund consistently places it in the top decile of equity funds. Please refer to Figure 7–10.

This fund has a downside (Morningstar) risk of 0.62, and the Sharpe ratio is 1.87, which makes this fund one of the most productive funds available. The expense ratio is 0.60, and the turnover is 53 percent.

Westwood Equity Retail

The manager of this fund for the last 10 years has been Susan Byrne. It is a Large Cap Value Fund. The 10-year record is 13.7 percent compounded; the 5-year record is 17.8 percent compounded. That is 35 and 140 basis points better than the S&P 500. The downside (Morningstar) risk is 0.58, and the Sharpe ratio is 1.95. The Sharpe ratio makes this fund the best of the best in terms of reward-versus-risk productivity (Figure 7–11).

The expense ratio is 1.50, and the turnover is 106 percent. A turnover this high triggers a look at the tax consequences. Assume 39.6 percent for the tax rate on ordinary income and 28 percent for a tax rate on capital gain. An after-tax return for the 10-year period is 8.66 percent. That gives a tax efficiency of $(8.66/13.72) \times 100 = 63$ percent. The tax efficiency for the Vanguard Index 500 is 75 percent. This fund is a candidate for an IRA.

FIGURE 7-10

Robert Marchin: MAS Value Institutional

MAS Value Instl
Release Date: 06-30-97

EQ Style	FI Style	Morningstar Category
⊞ Large/Value	-	Mid-Cap Value

Performance: Trailing Periods

◉ Total Return %
○ Return in Dollars

Range of returns for Category

Fund

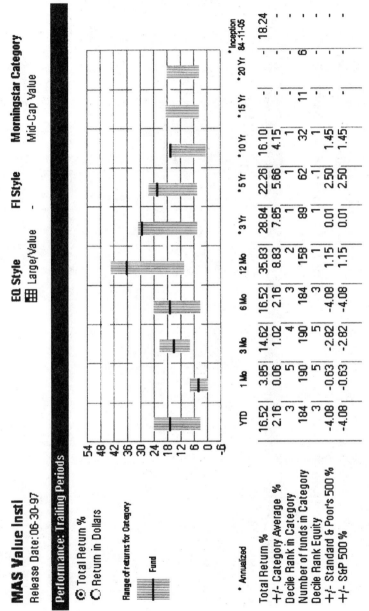

	YTD	1 Mo	3 Mo	6 Mo	12 Mo	*3 Yr	*5 Yr	*10 Yr	*15 Yr	*20 Yr	*Inception 84-11-05
Total Return %	16.52	3.85	14.62	16.52	35.83	28.84	22.26	16.10	-	-	18.24
+/- Category Average %	2.16	0.06	1.02	2.16	8.83	7.85	5.66	4.15	-	-	-
Decile Rank in Category	3	5	4	3	2	1	1	1	-	-	-
Number of funds in Category	184	190	190	184	158	89	62	32	11	6	-
Decile Rank Equity	3	5	5	3	1	1	1	1	-	-	-
+/- Standard & Poor's 500 %	-4.08	-0.63	-2.82	-4.08	1.15	0.01	2.50	1.45	-	-	-
+/- S&P 500 %	-4.08	-0.63	-2.82	-4.08	1.15	0.01	2.50	1.45	-	-	-

* Annualized

Source: Morningstar Principia.

FIGURE 7-11

Susan Byrne: Westwood Equity Retail

Westwood Equity Ret
Release Date: 06-30-97

EQ Style	FI Style	Morningstar Category
⊞ Large/Blend	-	Large Blend

Performance: Trailing Periods

◉ Total Return %
○ Return in Dollars

Range of returns for Category
▓ Fund

*Annualized	YTD	1 Mo	3 Mo	6 Mo	12 Mo	*3 Yr	*5 Yr	*10 Yr	*15 Yr	*20 Yr	*Inception 87-01-02
Total Return %	18.49	5.78	15.53	18.49	32.40	28.84	22.37	14.04	-	-	15.58
+/- Category Average %	1.79	1.77	0.21	1.79	3.64	4.43	4.99	1.41	-	-	-
Decile Rank in Category	4	1	6	4	3	1	1	3	-	-	-
Number of funds in Category	662	678	676	662	626	420	247	134	91	83	-
Decile Rank Equity	2	2	4	2	2	1	1	3	-	-	-
+/- Standard & Poor's 500 %	-2.11	1.30	-1.91	-2.11	-2.28	0.01	2.61	-0.61	-	-	-
+/- S&P 500 %	-2.11	1.30	-1.91	-2.11	-2.28	0.01	2.61	-0.61	-	-	-

Source: Morningstar Principia.

Clipper

The lead manager on this fund is James Gipson, and the comanager is Michael Sandler. The average manager tenure is 8 years. This is a Large Cap Value Fund. Figure 7–12 shows a 10-year record of 14.03 percent and a 5-year record of 17.93 percent. That is 66 and 152 basis points better than the S&P 500.

The 3-year downside (Morningstar) risk is 0.75, and the Sharpe ratio is 1.60. The expense ratio is 1.08, and the turnover is 24 percent. Gibson and his team members believe in concentration. The fund has 19 holdings, and the top 10 represent 81 percent of the total assets.

Vanguard/Primecap

This is a Large Cap Core Fund. The lead manager is Howard Schow and the comanagers are Theo Kolokotrones and Joel Fried. The average manager tenure is 5 years. Figure 7–13 shows the record of accomplishment. The 1-year return is 13.4 percent, and the 5-year return is 19.4 percent. That is 1 and 299 basis points better than the S&P 500.

The 3-year downside (Morningstar) risk is 0.93, and the Sharpe ratio is 1.39. The turnover of this fund is only 10 percent, and the expense ratio is 0.59.

ACTIVE MANAGER SELECTION

Let us review the key features that I have covered so far because they are some of the characteristics I look at before I put a fund on my buy list.

CONSISTENT, LONG-TERM RETURN

Academics typically say that past performance has no bearing on future performance. I am from the school of prag-

FIGURE 7-12

James Gipson: Clipper

Clipper
Release Date: 06-30-97

EQ Style	FI Style	Morningstar Category
Large/Value	-	Large Value

Performance: Trailing Periods

○ Total Return %
○ Return in Dollars

Range of returns for Category

Fund

*Annualized

	YTD	1 Mo	3 Mo	6 Mo	12 Mo	*3 Yr	*5 Yr	*10 Yr	*15 Yr	*20 Yr	*Inception 84-02-29
Total Return %	17.92	3.52	14.19	17.92	27.11	27.85	20.04	15.59	-	-	17.50
+/- Category Average %	2.49	-0.21	0.53	2.49	-1.38	4.89	3.09	3.82	-	-	-
Decile Rank in Category	3	7	5	3	7	1	2	1	-	-	-
Number of funds in Category	290	293	293	290	266	168	108	54	32	26	-
Decile Rank Equity	2	6	6	2	4	1	2	2	-	-	-
+/- Standard & Poor's 500 %	-2.68	-0.96	-3.25	-2.68	-7.57	-0.98	0.28	0.94	-	-	-
+/- S&P 500 %	-2.68	-0.96	-3.25	-2.68	-7.57	-0.98	0.28	0.94	-	-	-

Source: Morningstar Principia.

FIGURE 7-13

Howard Schow: Vanguard/Primecap

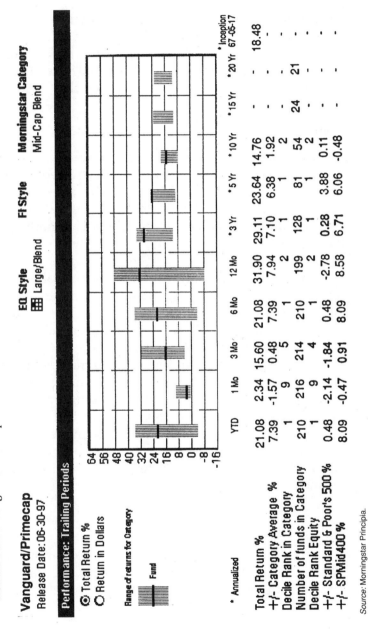

Vanguard/Primecap
Release Date: 06-30-97

EQ Style
Large/Blend

Ft Style

Morningstar Category
Mid-Cap Blend

Performance: Trailing Periods

○ Total Return %
○ Return in Dollars

Range of returns for Category

Fund

* Annualized	YTD	1 Mo	3 Mo	6 Mo	12 Mo	*3 Yr	*5 Yr	*10 Yr	*15 Yr	*20 Yr	*Inception 67-05-17
Total Return %	21.08	2.34	15.60	21.08	31.90	29.11	23.64	14.76	–	–	18.48
+/- Category Average %	7.39	-1.57	0.48	7.39	7.94	7.10	6.38	1.92	–	–	–
Decile Rank in Category	1	9	5	1	2	1	1	2	–	–	–
Number of funds in Category	210	216	214	210	199	128	81	54	24	21	–
Decile Rank Equity	1	9	4	1	2	1	1	2	–	–	–
+/- Standard & Poor's 500 %	0.48	-2.14	-1.84	0.48	-2.78	0.28	3.88	0.11	–	–	–
+/- SPMid400 %	8.09	-0.47	0.91	8.09	8.58	6.71	6.06	-0.48	–	–	–

Source: Morningstar Principia.

177

matism and hard knocks. Let us suppose that I am the manager of a baseball team. It is the ninth inning. Our team is at bat and is behind by 1 run. I would rather have a lifetime 0.300 hitter at the plate than a lifetime 0.100 hitter. I suspect that most of you reading this book would feel the same way.

TENURE

I prefer a manager with a consistent, long-term record of accomplishment. Most of the funds I just covered have that characteristic. I also am willing to give a new manager a chance to succeed if one or both of the following exists. First, the manager may have a great record at another firm. If the style he or she plans to use at the new firm is fundamentally the same as the old, I give a favorable weighting to the past record. For example, I felt that way about Mary Lisanti as she moved from Evergreen to Bankers Trust to Strong. (I typically put my small-cap asset class in the IRA of a client. Otherwise, following Mary around could get to be expensive on an after-tax basis.)

Second, I give favorable weighting if the new manager was a comanager but not the lead manager and plans to follow the playbook that is in place and working. For example, Shelby Davis had a distinguished record at Davis NY Venture A Fund. Christopher Davis comanaged the fund starting in October 1995. Shelby stepped down from this fund in February 1997. So far, Christopher seems to follow the same playbook.

EXPENSE RATIO

The level of the expense ratio of a fund is like a mirror. The mirror reflects the attitude of management. We do not see the attitude in the mirror; we see the result of the attitude.

The responsibility lies first with the *management of the fund company* and second with the *manager of the fund*.

> The level of the expense ratio of a fund is like a mirror. The mirror reflects the attitude of management.

Figure 5–8 presents compelling evidence about expense ratios. The odds are that a fund with a high expense ratio will not do as well as a fund with a low expense ratio. Some fund managers are in tune with this need. Many are not. Many simply take the stance that it is out of their control.

I find that fund managers who are "owners" often pay more attention to expenses than do nonowners. As used here, an "owner" is a principal that also acts as a fund manager. I also include in this definition those fund managers who may not be principals but still put a substantial portion of their personal assets and cash flow into the fund that they manage. An expression describes this behavior: Fund managers that "eat their own cooking" have a heightened sensitivity to fund expenses. I prefer managers who do this. It means that they are on the same side of the table as shareholders, that is, my clients.

Fund managers that do not fit my "owner" definition should, nonetheless, care about expenses. It comes out of the pocket of the shareholder. Shareholders and their advisors vote with their feet. They can look for another fund where the attitude about expenses is more businesslike.

TURNOVER

Turnover costs are not included in the expense ratio. I said earlier that high turnover means increased transaction costs. These include brokerage commissions and the spread between bid and ask prices for the underlying securities.

TAX EFFICIENCY

Common sense says that higher turnover means higher tax costs. Yes, no, and maybe. The key is the degree to which a manager makes the effort to offset gains and losses. A few managers I spoke with waxed eloquent when asked this question. Many give an answer that is not so eloquent. Some even sound like they make it up as they speak.

ADDITIONAL FEATURES

When I evaluate a fund manager, there are other items that I also consider important: concentration and composition.

Concentration

Remember the colorful quote from Warren Buffett about diversification? Look at Figure 7–14. This shows the record of U.S. Diversified Equity Funds grouped by the number of names in the portfolio. Figure 7–15 shows the portion of the portfolio that is in the top 10 holdings. You need both of these numbers to define holding concentration. The reason is that some managers use the farm system approach. Peter Lynch was an example. He typically had more than 1,000 names in his fund, but most were there in token amounts just so he could watch them and receive company reports.

The data in Figures 7–14 and 7–15 show that funds with the largest number of holdings have the greatest return. It is just the opposite of Buffett's comment! Is Buffett right or wrong? He is right. (Did you expect me to say otherwise?) I must, however, paraphrase his comment in view of Figures 7–14 and 7–15. Here is my interpretation of Buffett's comment, applied to mutual fund managers: If you concentrate your holdings, you had better be right. Having a limited number of holdings magnifies the error if

FIGURE 7-14

U.S. Diversified Equity Funds: Grouped by Total Holdings

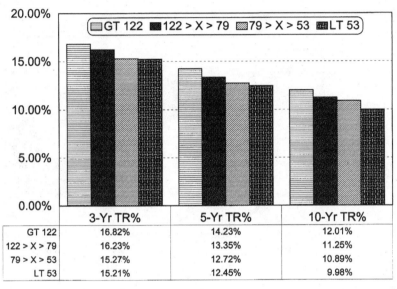

	3-Yr TR%	5-Yr TR%	10-Yr TR%
GT 122	16.82%	14.23%	12.01%
122 > X > 79	16.23%	13.35%	11.25%
79 > X > 53	15.27%	12.72%	10.89%
LT 53	15.21%	12.45%	9.98%

Data Source: Morningstar Principia.

you are wrong. Otherwise, your odds are better with diversification.

Some managers do concentrate successfully. Instead of carpet bombing using the laws of large numbers, they prefer surgical strikes using laser-guided bombs. Look again at the discussion of the managers listed earlier in this chapter. George Mairs III and Ronald Canakaris both use a concentrated approach. The framers of the Lexington Corporate Leaders fund believed in concentration. Bill Ruane and Richard Cunniff at Sequoia do also.

There is one other point to consider about concentra-

FIGURE 7–15

U.S. Diversified Equity Funds: Grouped by Top 10 Holdings, Percent

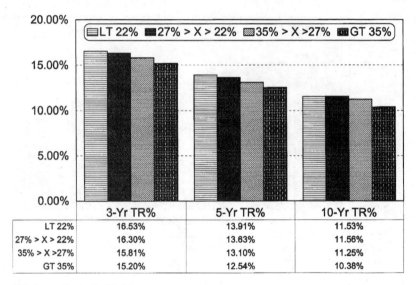

	3-Yr TR%	5-Yr TR%	10-Yr TR%
LT 22%	16.53%	13.91%	11.53%
27% > X > 22%	16.30%	13.63%	11.56%
35% > X >27%	15.81%	13.10%	11.25%
GT 35%	15.20%	12.54%	10.38%

Data Source: Morningstar Principia.

tion. Some managers may have an average number of names in the portfolio but limit the bulk of their holdings to one or two industries. Sector funds are easy to find. I am talking here about funds with a "Diversified Equity" label. As I write this, there are 10 "diversified" funds with a 50 percent or greater concentration in financials. There are 24 "diversified" funds with a 50 percent or greater concentration in technology. One should not reach a judgment about a manager based on this information alone. There are some good managers among those 34 funds. William Ruane and Richard Cunniff at Sequoia and Marty Whitman at Third Avenue Value are examples.

Composition

Composition is another aspect to understand. Let us suppose we have a U.S. Equity Fund under review. We want to know what else is in the portfolio. How much is in foreign stocks? A manager that does well at picking stocks in the U.S. market is not automatically qualified to do well at picking foreign stocks. How much is in multinationals with heavy foreign activities? Heavy foreign content can cause the fund to behave in ways that you did not expect. It can also impair your ability to manage the risk of the overall portfolio. You want asset classes with the lowest correlations with each other as possible.

How much is in cash equivalents or bonds? Mutual fund managers typically carry between 5 and 10 percent of the fund in cash to handle redemptions. If it is substantially higher than that, it is either good news or bad news. The manager may have a strong belief and conviction about his or her strategy and buy discipline. He or she may face a situation with high levels of incoming cash and a dearth of good buy candidates. I view that as good news. I prefer managers who stay with what they know and do best. On the other hand, the manager may see an apparition that tells him or her to get out of the market. I view that as bad news—unless, of course, I see the same apparition. (Just kidding.) How do I tell which is the true motivation? I have the best batting average on this question in cases in which I can speak with the fund manager. I listen carefully to the answer. If the focus of the response is on the lack of good buy candidates, I have a likely answer.

What if the portion in cash has a minus sign in front? This typically means that the manager makes use of margin debt. Like concentration, there is nothing wrong with margin as long as you know what you are doing. As I write this, there are 26 funds with a negative cash position. When you see this negative cash, look next at the portion in stocks. If they use margin, this figure is typically greater than 100 percent.

How much is in that mystery category called "other"? If the column labeled "other" has a large number, you should probe deeper. A fund-of-funds has a large number in this column. There may be other things going on here. "Other" may be something tame like convertibles, preferreds, or warrants.

"Other" may mean exotics like derivatives or private securities that may be illiquid. That raises a red flag for me. When I see a large number in the "other" column, I read the prospectus again to find out how much latitude the manager has. With some funds, like Rydex Nova and Rydex Ursa, you can see the exotics up there in bright lights. It is what they do. You know what to expect if you decide to buy it.

For some funds, it is harder to detect. Exotics are part of a lengthy list found in the prospectus. The list shows permissible security types. It can include exotics. When invoked, they may cause the fund to behave in a manner that is quite different from the asset class included in your portfolio design. Here is my rule: If it is not obvious, ask. Speak with someone knowledgeable at the fund—preferably the fund manager. Find out what is in the "other" column. If the manager cannot articulate a strategy for the use of "other" in plain English, then move on.

MANAGER STYLE: WHAT IS IT?

Let us agree on some basic concepts. Manager style describes the characteristics of the portfolio resulting from manager actions. The result may or may not be consistent with the intended result articulated in the prospectus. In the world of equities, the basic idea of growth and value, of large and small stocks, has been around for many years. The idea of relating manager style to an asset subclass has been around only for a single decade. Some of the earliest work on this second point came through the efforts of William Sharpe. He published two articles, one in 1988[3] and the other in 1992.[4] Sharpe found that manager style is the overwhelming factor in explaining variations in manager returns. In addition, Robert Ludwig of SEI Asset Management and others found that the tendency of styles to drift accounted for much of their underperformance relative to their benchmarks.[5]

Think about the implications of what you just read. Let us assume that we construct a portfolio of managers with a high correlation to their style benchmarks and with diversification of styles. Then we construct a second portfolio with managers who engage in style rotation or have marketlike characteristics. The work of Ludwig and others suggests that the first portfolio is likely to outperform the second.

It is likely that you saw charts like those in Figures 7–16 and 7–17.[6] They are indices that show what we learned in Investments 101. Over the long term, small stocks outperform large stocks, and value stocks outperform growth stocks. There is something else going on here that is not so obvious.

3. William F. Sharpe, "Determining a Fund's Effective Asset Mix," *Investment Management Review,* November/December 1988, pp. 59–69.
4. William F. Sharpe, "Asset Allocation: Management Style and Performance Measurement," *The Journal of Portfolio Management*, vol. 18, no. 2, Winter 1992.
5. Robert S. Ludwig, "The Inefficiency of Indexed Portfolios and the Evidence for Active Management," *Personal Financial Planning*, Warren, Gorham & Lamont, March/April 1996.
6. Approval for use of BARRA index given by James Branscome, Senior Vice President of Standard & Poor's.

FIGURE 7–16

Large Stocks Versus Small Stocks: Initial Investment of $1

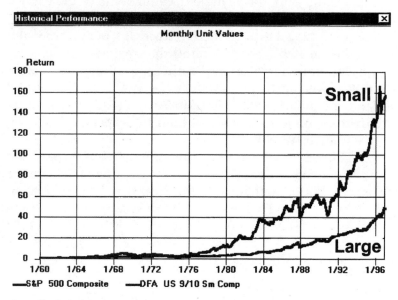

Source: Frontier Analytics, Inc.
Data Source: Standard & Poor's, Wilshire Associates, Inc., and Dimensional Fund Advisors.

Let us consider another metaphor. Some of the world-class masters of communication and imagery are in the advertising industry. One of my favorites is a television commercial photographed aboard a cruise ship. The people in the picture sit in their deck chairs with a sleepy look on their face. Then there is an announcement. A voice says that there is a certain brand of coffee now being served in the starboard lounge. The people rise from their chairs and walk briskly. The next shot is a view of the stern of the ship. It shows the ship tilted to the starboard. The image instantly

F I G U R E   7–17

Growth Stocks Versus Value Stocks: Initial Investment of $1

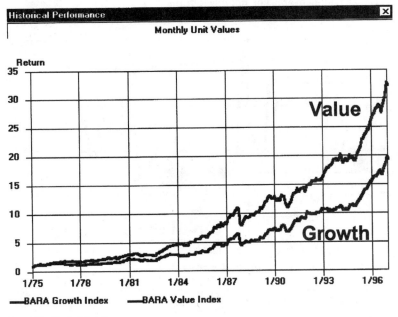

Source: Frontier Analytics, Inc.
Data Source: BARRA and Standard & Poor's.

created is that everyone aboard the ship went immediately to the starboard lounge to drink the coffee.

Now look at Figures 7–18 and 7–19.[7] These show the same indices as before but in a different context. Each graph shows the excess return of one index over the other. When the excess return line is above the centerline in Figure 7–18,

---

7. Approval for use of BARRA index given by James Branscome, Senior Vice
    President of Standard & Poor's.

FIGURE 7–18

Large Stocks Versus Small Stocks, Excess Returns:
1-Year Rolling Average of Monthly Returns

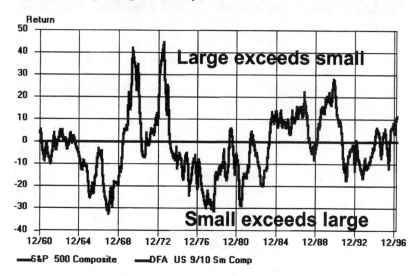

Source: Frontier Analytics, Inc.
Data Source: Standard & Poor's, Wilshire Associates, Inc., and Dimensional Fund Advisors.

large does better than small. When the excess return line in
Figure 7–19 is above the centerline, growth does better than
value. Notice that this excess return line moves up and
down like a wave. It is as if the coffee service were alternat-
ing between the starboard lounge and the port lounge. The
problem is that you never know in advance which lounge is
serving that day. There are times when one style is in fashion or favor followed by the other style.

Why does this happen? I am not aware of any study
that proves with certainty the reason for this phenomenon.

FIGURE 7–19

Growth Stocks Versus Value Stocks, Excess Returns:
1-Year Rolling Average of Monthly Returns

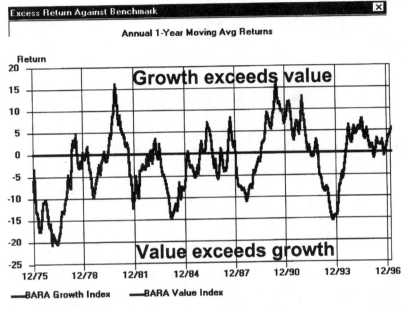

Source: Frontier Analytics, Inc.
Data Source: BARRA and Standard & Poor's.

I suppose that it is difficult because investor psychology has so much to do with what is fashionable. Damn the torpedoes and don't confuse me with the facts are familiar attitudes. Perhaps the words *euphoria* and *despair* had their roots in the stock market. No? Well, it sure seems like it at times. The point of this is *not* to prove why it happens but to recognize that it does happen. After we recognize that, we can tailor a strategy to take advantage of the behavior.

CHAPTER 8

Classifying and Using Manager Style

PORTFOLIO METHOD

How do we identify the style of the manager? By reading the prospectus? Most of them give the manager so much latitude that it is hard to depend on it to pinpoint a style. What about listening to the manager? That is an improvement over the prospectus. I usually find a way to talk with or, at least listen to, the manager of the fund in which I have an interest. Is that enough? No, it is not enough.

The best way is to refer back to my legal metaphor and look at the evidence. I spoke about direct evidence and circumstantial evidence. There are two methods on the scene today to assist in assessing the style of a manager. One way is to look under the hood at the portfolio holdings. Find out the characteristics of the underlying securities individually and as a group. Most people refer to this as the *portfolio method* of manager analysis. I think of it as *direct evidence* in the legal metaphor.

As I write this, the mutual fund reporting service with the most depth in the portfolio method is Morningstar. They have a large number of analysts who spend their time exercising the portfolio method. Other reporting services such as ValueLine also provide portfolio information on the mutual funds that they cover.

Look at Figure 8–1. This is a model developed by Morningstar to differentiate mutual fund manager styles. They call it their "style box." On the left side, they have a differentiation by the median market capitalization of the holdings of the fund. Across the top, they have a differentiation by the relative price-earnings ratio plus the relative

FIGURE 8–1

Morningstar: Equity Style Box, Portfolio Method

Valuation Method

Market Capitalization ↓	Value Low (Rel PE+Rel PB)	Blend	Growth High (Rel PE+Rel PB)
Large >$5B			
Medium <$5B, >$1B			
Small <$1B			

Size

Data Source: Morningstar Principia.

FIGURE 8–2

Mutual Fund Average Returns by Manager Style Box, Market
Capitalization

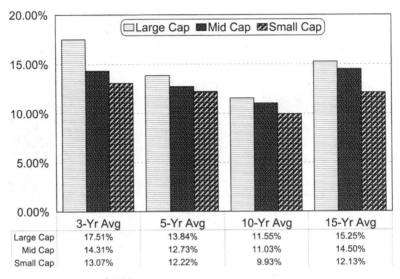

	3-Yr Avg	5-Yr Avg	10-Yr Avg	15-Yr Avg
Large Cap	17.51%	13.84%	11.55%	15.25%
Mid Cap	14.31%	12.73%	11.03%	14.50%
Small Cap	13.07%	12.22%	9.93%	12.13%

Data Source: Morningstar Principia.

price-book ratio. It is relative in the sense that it compares
the ratios of the fund to the ratios of the underlying benchmark such as the S&P 500 Stock Index.

Now look at Figure 8–2. It shows average returns for
U.S. Domestic Equity Funds taking horizontal slices from
the style box. It shows that Large Cap Funds beat Small Cap
Funds on the average over the last 3, 5, 10, and 15 years.
Why not just buy Large Cap? Be careful about falling into
this trap. You never know when they will serve the coffee
on the other side of the ship. Remember, over the long haul,
small stocks perform better than large stocks.

FIGURE 8-3

Mutual Fund Average Returns by Manager Style Box, Valuation Method

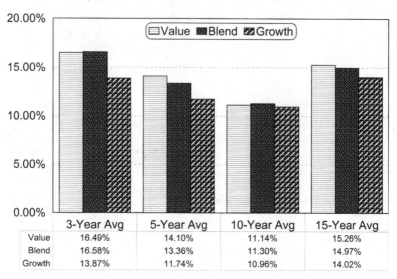

	3-Year Avg	5-Year Avg	10-Year Avg	15-Year Avg
Value	16.49%	14.10%	11.14%	15.26%
Blend	16.58%	13.36%	11.30%	14.97%
Growth	13.87%	11.74%	10.96%	14.02%

Data Source: Morningstar Principia.

Next, look at Figure 8–3. This is a summary of U.S. Domestic Equity Funds taking vertical slices from the style box. It shows that value funds beat growth funds over the last 3, 5, 10, and 15 years. There is nothing surprising here.

RETURNS METHOD

The second way to analyze the style of a manager is to look at the evidence by the *indirect method*. Lawyers and judges refer to this as *circumstantial evidence*. The term applied most often to this approach is *manager analysis by the returns method.* Another phrase used often is *returns-based style analysis,* or *factor analysis,* and the creator of this technique is William Sharpe (see footnotes 3 and 4 in this chapter). The returns method regresses the periodic returns of a manager with the returns of specified indices of related financial assets. I find it helpful to look for confirmation or divergence between the portfolio method and the returns method. I also find that using both methods helps me to have better aim to properly assign a manager to a style and to detect drift away from that style. You may also find some differences in the approach used here from those you saw elsewhere. Let me use two analogies to put the returns method in perspective.

OIL AND GAS WELL LOG

I worked during the summer to pay for part of my college expenses. One summer I worked on an oil-drilling rig. How do the people drilling the well know if they have oil or gas down the hole? The person responsible for this determination is a geologist. First, they analyze the rock cuttings coming out of the hole while drilling is in progress. You might think of this as direct evidence. They also ask one of the servicing companies to *run a log.* To do that, they lower an instrument with electronic probes into the hole. They tether the instrument at the end of a cable made of material suitable for conducting an electronic signal back to the surface. A recording device records the signal on a continuously moving strip of paper. Without getting too technical, if the signal swings away from the centerline, it suggests the presence of oil or gas. You might think of this as indirect, or circumstantial, evidence suggesting the presence or absence of oil or gas.

ELECTROCARDIOGRAM

Your family doctor gives you a physical exam. They look at direct evidence such as the appearance of various parts of your body, your ability to speak with logic and clarity, and your physical movements and coordination. They also consider indirect or circumstantial evidence. One tool for gathering this indirect evidence is an *electrocardiograph,* which is an instrument used in the detection and diagnosis of heart abnormalities. It measures electrical potentials on the body surface and generates a record of the electrical currents associated with heart muscle activity. The physician analyzes the record and makes use of the results to assist in the overall assessment of the state of your health.

The drilling log and the electrocardiogram analogies have a few things in common. First, they both use *inference* to reflect what is happening. You can think of this as *indirect,* or *circumstantial, evidence.* Second, the geologist and the doctor *do not rely on this technique alone* to reach a judgment. They refer to other corroborating physical or direct evidence. Third, nobody expects the geologists or the doctors to be proficient at interpreting the results of these indirect methods the first time they try it. *It takes months, perhaps years, before there is competence.* Each of these points seems appropriate for manager analysis by the returns method as well.

MANAGER STYLE

Now let us apply this logic to the analysis of manager style and put this discussion in perspective. Morningstar performs a valuable service for advisors and sophisticated investors through detailed manager analysis by the portfolio method. That is one reason they are the leaders in their field. As I see it, manager style analysis using the portfolio method is like direct evidence. It is *vital information*. Manager style analysis using the returns method is like indirect, or circumstantial, evidence. It is *too early* for me to declare it as *vital*. At this point, I find it helpful as *a confirming tool*. I see the two approaches as *complementary* and *corroborating*, not as alternatives. When I find divergence between the two, it is a flag for me to dig deeper. For example, I try additional or different benchmarks, or I ask the manager directly what is happening with the portfolio.

HISTORICALLY SIGNIFICANT BATTLES

To understand this issue better, I find it useful to study some of the great battles in the history of the planet. There are many to choose from, but a few immediately come to mind. There was the Battle of Waterloo, the Battle of Gettysburg, and the Battle of Midway. Then there is the Chicago Donnybrook. What? You did not hear about that one? Well, you may still be in luck. You may be at least able to read the transcript. Furthermore, it may still be in progress! At the last count, they were in the 92nd round. The combatants are two Chicago-based firms, Morningstar and Ibbotson Associates, Inc. I am talking here about a throwback to the days of bare-knuckles boxing. In the red corner, we have John Rekenthaler & Don Phillips of Morningstar. In the blue corner, we have Lori Lucas and Mark Riepe of Ibbotson Associates. It is part of an ongoing battle for the hearts and minds of investment advisors, consultants, sophisticated investors, and the media about the best way to assess mutual fund manager styles. In the interests of full disclosure, Morningstar is the industry leader in manager style analysis by the portfolio method. Ibbotson Associates, Inc., is an industry leader in manager style analysis using the Sharpe-developed, returns-based method.

John Rekenthaler says a few things about returns-based style analysis.[1]

Style analysis is fun, easy to use, colorful, and miscast.

The problem is, style analysis raises questions it cannot answer. It falls silent about fund styles when such information is most needed—with flexibly run funds. When monitoring portfolio adjustments, its signals are slow and unreliable. And, in spotlighting portfolio managers whose funds have performed terrifically, the technique commits the very mistake it was created to avoid: it confuses a style's and a manager's effects. Ultimately, style analysis is only as valuable as the fundamental research that it inspires.

Style analysis appeals to vendors because it doesn't require fund portfolios.

Style analysis does help in tracking private money managers, where information is limited, and it may aid highly advanced investors. As a primary fund-selection tool, though, it is a flop.

Here is a quote from Don Phillips of Morningstar.[2]

Lori Lucas (of Ibbotson) held up Sequoia funds and said, well, it has a low R-squared and so this is not really a fund you can analyze using factor analysis. Then the next day, Gary Miller told an audience, well, this really doesn't work well with Fidelity's funds, because the managers change quite a bit. If you're embracing a system that can't incorporate Sequoia and Fidelity Magellan and Fidelity Contra

---

1. John Rekenthaler, "Style Analysis: I and II," *Morningstar Principia Commentaries*, February 16, 1996, and March 1, 1996.
2. Don Phillips, "Factor Analysis: Are You Getting the True Portfolio Picture?" by Robert N. Veres, *Journal of Financial Planning*, February 1996, pp. 30–37.

funds, how in the world is that going to help you select the best mutual funds for your clients?

Lori Lucas and Mark Riepe of Ibbotson Associates, Inc., say a few things in rebuttal.[3]

> Like all forms of analysis, returns-based style analysis is only as "intelligent" as the data-input choices and the analytical skills of those that use it.

> The author of the paper wondered why the results were so far off from those of fundamental analysis. The answer is simple: improperly applied analysis.

> Of course, the instability of results that accompanies poor implementation and interpretation is a problem that plagues all of investment analysis whether it is quantitative in nature or not.

> Again, referring to a survey of the December 1995 release of Morningstar's OnDisc we find that the average U.S. Diversified equity fund shows an R^2 of 65 percent when compared to broad benchmarks such as the S&P 500. When using returns-based style analysis, however, the average R^2 rises to 86 percent.

Now you know why historians may place the Chicago Donnybrook in the list of the greatest battles of all time.

SHORTCOMINGS OF BOTH METHODS

I am a bit more sanguine than the combatants. I have worked with both methods. As I see it, both methods have benefits and shortcomings. Here are two among many suggested areas requiring improvement: time delay and sensitivity to the benchmarks used.

---

3. Lori Lucas, CFA, and Mark W. Riepe, Vice President, Web Page, http://www.ibbotson.inter.net/welcome.htm, Ibbotson Associates, Inc.

TIME DELAY

The first is the problem of time delay. A search of Morningstar Principia (March 1997 data) reveals 2,168 U.S. Diversified Equity Funds with portfolio dates. The earliest date is April 1995, and the most recent is March 1997. The median is October 1996. The CD arrived at my office in mid-April. We are talking 6 months. For some funds it is as bad as 12 months. In fairness, much of this problem is out of the control of Morningstar. Most fund managers report only on the frequency required by the Securities and Exchange Commission, that is, 60 days after the close of the fiscal year and fiscal half-year. The fund managers do not want their competitors to know their holdings any sooner than necessary. Morningstar can only persuade and cajole the fund managers to report with improved timeliness and frequency. Here is an idea that I came up with to solve this problem. If the manager fails to report on time, deduct one star from his or her rating. If the manager reports quarterly, reward him or her by adding one star. If the report is monthly, add two stars. I am just kidding, of course. On the other hand,...

The returns method has a problem of time delay as well. That includes the style analyzer illustrated in this book. The style history shown here is a rolling average of style class exposure. It gives a broad historical view of the level of style consistency in the portfolio. Each point on a style history shown in this book is an *economic representation* of what happened at the midpoint of the 12-month period, or 6 months ago.

I started testing the returns method several months ago. I usually run both a 1-year and a 3-year averaging analysis to make a comparison. Sharpe used a 3-year period in his 1992 paper referenced in Chapter 7. I only show here the 1-year averaging method. Using the 1-year method instead of the 3-year method is like turning up the sensitivity on the recording device for the oil-well logging instrument or the electrocardiograph. The long-term-history chart displays the added sensitivity for 1-year averaging compared with 3-year averaging. That compares favorably with what you would expect and the nature of the mathematics of averaging. Try plotting returns using a spreadsheet calculation of both 3-year and 1-year averaging. You can see the sensitivity difference there.

For me, the added sensitivity is okay, even preferable. I make that tradeoff in order to get the 6-month look back afforded by the 1-year averaging method. Besides, I can *zoom in* on a period that I wish to review in more detail. For the illustrations shown in the first example, I have a long-term view of history (starting in 1984) and a more recent portion of the graph (starting in 1994). The actual calculation starts 1 year earlier than this in each case.

Over the months of testing, I ran both 36-six month and 12-month averaging for each fund I analyzed. Some folks out there make use of a 36 months' averaging of returns. I find that gives a view of major trends. There are advantages to having that perspective, but the problem is that it is always 18 months out of date. There are also advantages of 1-year averaging. With it, I get greater sensitivity and a shorter look-back period. I see both of those as advantages.

By use of the 1-year method, do I sacrifice precision? Yes, but it is marginal in practical terms. First, I am typically not satisfied until I get over 90 percent style attribution in any case. Second, there is some degradation in "selection return" validity indicated by a reduction in the tracking error that mathematicians refer to as the *t-statistic*. However, a visual comparison of the excess cumulative returns graphs (such as Figure 8–18) typically shows the curves to be very close. Third, I insist on a minimum of 4 years of monthly data. Fourth, over months of day-to-day usage, I find that I get corroboration with the portfolio method with *far greater frequency* using 1-year averaging rather than 3-year averaging. I hope to do testing with weekly data in the near future. That offers the opportunity for a look-back period shorter than 6 months.

Time delay is an issue with the returns method. Bill Sharpe gave a talk at a conference in late 1996[4] in which he mentioned this problem. He said that he dampens the problem of time delay by applying greater weight to the most recent data points. An exponential average is one of many possible methods to do this. There is some discussion among users and providers about the use of daily data. Here is what Bill Sharpe said about daily data:

> The problem with daily returns is you're getting more and more noise. There's a problem here with noise, and the more noise you get, the poorer your estimates are.[5]

SENSITIVITY TO THE BENCHMARKS USED

There is a second issue here with the returns method. I have found that the results of the style analysis are at times sensitive to the choice of index used as a proxy for a particular style. Providers use a slightly different approach to compute their index. They reconstitute the index on different schedules. It is *critical* that you take the time to understand

---

4. William F. Sharpe, Speech at conference sponsored by Charles Schwab & Co., Inc., November 1996.
5. William F. Sharpe, "Setting the Record Straight on Style Analysis," Interviewer: Barry Vinocur, *Fee Advisor,* November/December 1995, pp. 48–56.

the rationale and methodology used by the provider. Take equity indices for example. Make sure that you understand the mathematical location of the boundary lines between market capitalization size categories. The same is true for valuation methods, that is, value and growth. Here is the point: If you do not understand the makeup of the bench-mark, how can you properly interpret the results of the analysis? I find that most providers are happy to supply that information. All you have to do is ask.

APPLICATION OF MANAGER STYLE ANALYSIS

Next, I want to walk through two illustrations of manager analysis using both the portfolio method and the returns method. I selected an equity fund and a fixed-income fund. The equity fund is Fidelity Contrafund. The fixed-income fund is Scudder Income. I purposely selected these two funds because of manager change, style change, or both. Fidelity Contrafund has both, and Scudder Income has style change. You might look on this as a quick *stress test* of the methodology.

FIDELITY CONTRAFUND

Background
The manager of this fund since October 1990 has been Will Danoff. Preceding Will was Alan Leifer from 1984 until 1989 and Jeffrey Vinick (who moved on to Magellan). Figure 8–4 shows that this fund is in the top decile among equity funds for the last 5, 10, and 15 years. For the latest 3 years, how-ever, the ranking dropped to the third decile. Figure 8–5 shows the average portfolio turnover to be 246 percent. That means a holding period of roughly 5 months.

FIGURE 8-4

Fidelity Contrafund: Manager Analysis

Fidelity Contrafund
Release Date: 06-30-97

	EQ Style	FI Style	Morningstar Category
	Large/Blend	-	Mid-Cap Blend

Performance: Trailing Periods

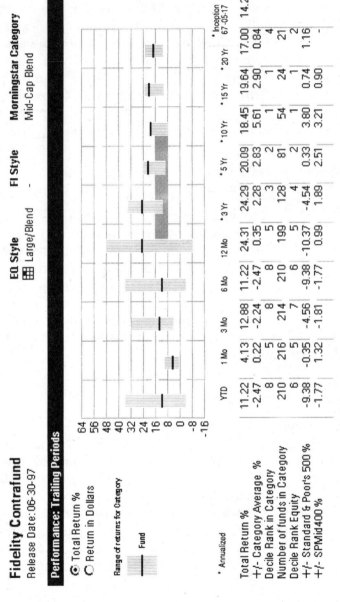

○ Total Return %
○ Return in Dollars

Range of returns for Category
▬ Fund

* Annualized

	YTD	1 Mo	3 Mo	6 Mo	12 Mo	*3 Yr	*5 Yr	*10 Yr	*15 Yr	*20 Yr	*Inception 67-05-17
Total Return %	11.22	4.13	12.88	11.22	24.31	24.29	20.09	18.45	19.64	17.00	14.26
+/- Category Average %	-2.47	0.22	-2.24	-2.47	0.35	2.28	2.83	5.61	2.90	0.84	-
Decile Rank in Category	8	5	8	8	5	3	2	1	1	4	-
Number of funds in Category	210	216	214	210	199	128	81	54	24	21	-
Decile Rank Equity	6	5	7	6	5	4	2	1	1	2	-
+/- Standard & Poor's 500 %	-9.38	-0.35	-4.56	-9.38	-10.37	-4.54	0.33	3.80	0.74	1.16	-
+/- SPMid400 %	-1.77	1.32	-1.81	-1.77	0.99	1.89	2.51	3.21	0.90	-	-

Source: Morningstar Principia.

FIGURE 8-5

Fidelity Contrafund: Manager Analysis, Portfolio Turnover

Fidelity Contrafund
Release Date: 03-31-97

EQ Style Large/Blend

FI Style -

Objective Growth

Performance: History

Turnover
● Fidelity Contrafund

Current Turnover Rate
-

Average Historical Turnover Rate
246

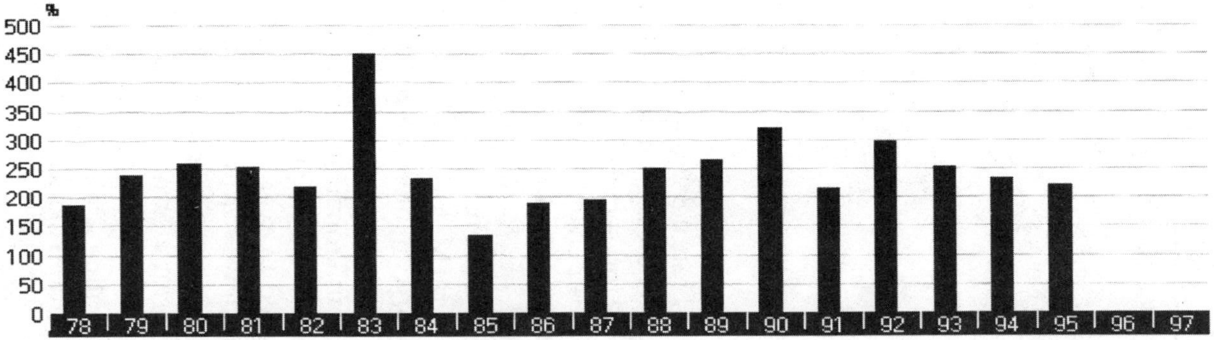

Source: Morningstar Principia.

FIGURE 8–6

Fidelity Contrafund: Manager Analysis, Concentration

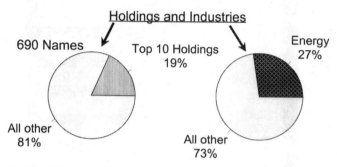

Holdings and Industries

690 Names   Top 10 Holdings   Energy
                     19%   27%

All other   All other
  81%   73%

Data Source: Morningstar Principia.

Figure 8–6 shows that Danoff holds 690 names. The top 10 holdings make up 19 percent of the portfolio. Energy is his top sector. That was not always the case. In 1994, he was 34 percent in high-tech stocks. Figure 8–7 shows 14 percent of the stock content is foreign stocks. In addition, a check of Morningstar Principia Advanced Analytics shows multinational stocks such as Schlumberger, IBM, and General Motors. Multinationals tend to give a portfolio a tilt toward an international behavior.

You can see from Figure 8–8 that this fund was roughly $330 million in size when Danoff took over in 1990. At that time, it had a small- to mid-cap style. Since then, it ballooned to over $24 billion in assets! Size is good news and bad news. Growth reflects high demand for the fund. That is good! It usually means that the manager produced a superior return. The bad news is that growth also means an ever-increasing struggle by the manager to maintain a buy discipline. Danoff had the following choices. He could (1) find more names, (2) take bigger stakes in current holdings,

F I G U R E 8–7

Fidelity Contrafund: Manager Analysis, Composition

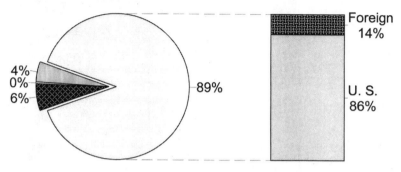

Check foreign content within U. S. stocks

☐Stocks ▥Bonds ▥Other ▨Cash

Data Source: Morningstar Principia.

or (3) execute a controlled drift to a large-cap style. He did all of the above. Part of the cap shift came from current holdings that grew up. He also brought large caps into the portfolio. For instance, Danoff made a bet on IBM in the early 1990s when there was blood in the streets of Armonk, figuratively speaking, of course. That paid off nicely for him. Peter Lynch did the same thing in dealing with size. He successfully made a large bet on Chrysler.

Figure 8–9 shows the manager style history according to Morningstar using the portfolio method. You can see there the shift to large cap starting in 1995. Now let us look at manager analysis using the returns method. First, let us look at a style history that covers all three managers. Then we will zoom in and focus just on the recent period of Danoff's time at the reins.

FIGURE 8-8

Fidelity Contrafund: Growth in Assets

Fidelity Contrafund
Release Date: 03-31-97

EQ Style
Large/Blend

FI Style
-

Objective
Growth

Performance: History

Net Assets

Current Net Assets ($mil)

Fidelity Contrafund

24969

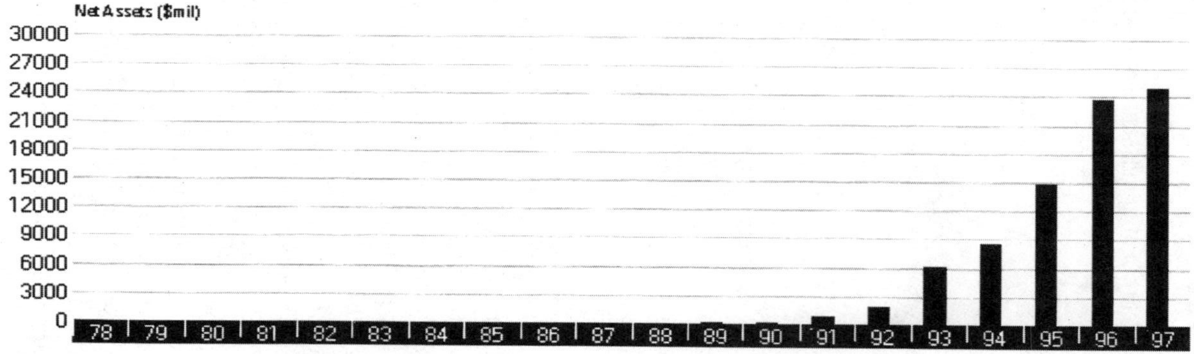

Net Assets ($mil)

Source: Morningstar Principia.

Fidelity Contrafund: Manager Analysis, Portfolio Holdings Method

Fidelity Contrafund
Release Date: 03-31-97

EQ Style
⊞ Large/Blend

FI Style
–

Objective
Growth

Portfolio: Stock Statistics

	Style	P/E	P/B	Price/ Cash Flow	5 Yr Earn Growth %	Return on Assets %	Debt % Total Cap	Median Mkt Cap ($mil)	Market Capitalization Breakdown %			
									Large >5 bil	Medium 1-5 bil	Small 250mil-1 bil	Micro Cap <250mil
As of 12-31-96	⊞	26.3	4.5	14.9	19.9	9.5	30.3	5126	–	–	–	–
3 year Average	–	23.8	3.7	14.9	13.9	8.9	29.4	4198	–	–	–	–
1996	–	26.6	3.7	13.8	15.7	8.3	34.3	5205	51.3	38.9	8.7	1.1
1995		22.3	4.1	16.9	17.5	10.0	25.4	4193	53.4	32.8	11.3	2.6
1994		22.5	3.5	14.1	8.5	8.6	28.5	3195	–	–	–	–
1993		27.8	4.2	16.5	9.3	7.7	28.7	2557	–	–	–	–
1992		21.4	2.4	–	2.5	4.2	39.0	3082	–	–	–	–
1991		–	–	–	–	–	–	–	–	–	–	–
1990		–	–	–	–	–	–	–	–	–	–	–
1989		–	–	–	–	–	–	–	–	–	–	–

Source: Morningstar Principia.

F I G U R E   8–10

Fidelity Contrafund: Returns Method Manager Analysis,
Style Benchmarks

Series	Start Year
Fidelity Contra Fund	1968
Frank Russell Co. 1000® Growth	1980
Frank Russell Co. 1000® Value	1980
Frank Russell Co. MidCap™	1980
Frank Russell Co. 2000® Growth	1980
Frank Russell Co. 2000® Value	1980

Source: Morningstar and Frank Russell Company.

Look at Figure 8–10. I chose the indices from Frank
Russell Company.[6] This chart shows the indices and the
time span of the data. The Russell Mid Cap Index overlaps
the Russell Large Cap Index in market cap to a limited

---

6. This book is not the appropriate forum for a detailed analysis of indices for
financial assets. It is critical for the advisor to know the definitions used
by each provider. *Growth/value* and *large/small* mean slightly different
things and have different ranges for Morningstar than for Frank Russell
Company or Wilshire Associates or BARRA or others. There is no standard set of definitions. You have to keep that in mind when you compare
results from Morningstar with those from the returns method using index
providers. Failure to heed this warning can result in inappropriate interpretation of manager analysis results.

degree.[7] To that extent, the choice of indices does not have the absolute purity described by Bill Sharpe as "mutually exclusive." I included the Russell Mid Cap Index[8] here because of Danoff's emphasis on mid-cap stocks in the early part of his tenure. He has many mid-cap holdings even as I write this. You may also notice in reading Sharpe's paper that he uses a standard set of 12 indices for the analysis of *all funds* illustrated in the paper. I prefer to have the least number of indices required to capture *the essence of the fund* and still reach an acceptable attribution percentage. If needed, I substitute or add manager style class indices until I raise the attribution above 80 percent, or, even better, above 90 percent. I want to focus only on those styles that are the *major contributors* to driving the returns of the fund.

Now look at Figure 8–11. Here I specify the calculation method. The first set of dates is the *style time period,* which is the date range to do the calculation. The *historical analysis range* lets me specify the rolling periods to average and the range of dates to display. An *in-sample benchmark* is an average calculated over the entire period. It does not account for changes in managers or style. An *out-of-sample benchmark* is dynamic. It is forward looking, and it reflects the latest style benchmark and adjusts for any changes in style. There is a repeat of this process for each 12-month rolling period. I typically use the *out-of-sample approach* as an aid to detect manager changes or style changes.

Figure 8–12 shows the calculation of the degree that the style benchmark explains the behavior of the fund. Ninety

7. The manager style indices provided by Wilshire Associates, Inc., also have a limited overlap in market cap.
8. As I write this, the Frank Russell Company does not offer a mid-cap index separated by growth and value styles.

F I G U R E 8–11

Fidelity Contrafund: Return Method Manager
Analysis, Calculation Method

percent of the returns of this fund have their explanation in
the style class chosen by the manager. Generally, any attribution above 80 percent is good and above 90 percent is
excellent. The other pie slice in Figure 8–12 has the label
"selection." I am uncomfortable with this label because it
draws a conclusion that may or may not be the case. When
I discuss this chart with a client, I say that the other 10 percent is *unexplained* by the movement of the style class. I say

FIGURE 8–12

Fidelity Contrafund: Returns Method Manager Analysis, Attribution from January 1983 Forward

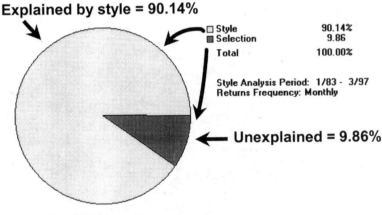

Explained by style = 90.14%

☐ Style	90.14%
◼ Selection	9.86
Total	100.00%

Style Analysis Period: 1/83 - 3/97
Returns Frequency: Monthly

⟵ Unexplained = 9.86%

Source: Frontier Analytics, Inc.

that it is most likely attributable to actions by the manager. For example, security selection can be one contributor. Market timing could be another. High concentration with a small number of names could be yet another. A heavy weighting in one or two industry sectors can be another. The use of specialized or illiquid securities could be another.

Now look at Figure 8–13.[9] This is the manager style history. I placed arrows to indicate the manager changes. The darker grays at the top of the graph reflect large cap. This chart includes mid-cap. Now look at Figure 8–14. This is a style map. The limit by the software is four quadrants by manager style. The earliest data point appears here as

9. See Figure 8–10 for definition of indices from Frank Russell Company.

Fidelity Contrafund: Returns Method Manager Analysis, Style History from 1984

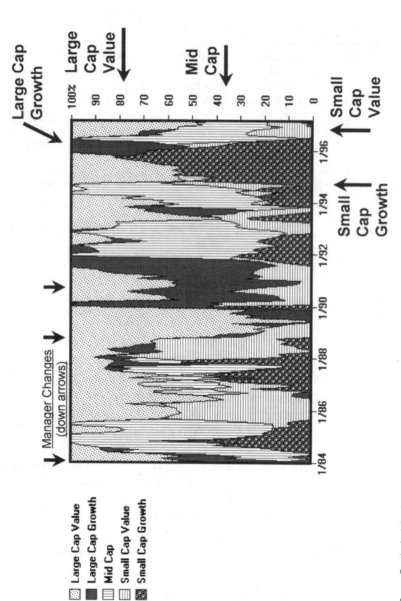

Large Cap Value
Large Cap Growth
Mid Cap
Small Cap Value
Small Cap Growth

Source: Frontier Analytics, Inc.

FIGURE 8–14

Fidelity Contrafund: Returns Method Manager Analysis, Style Map from January 1983 Forward

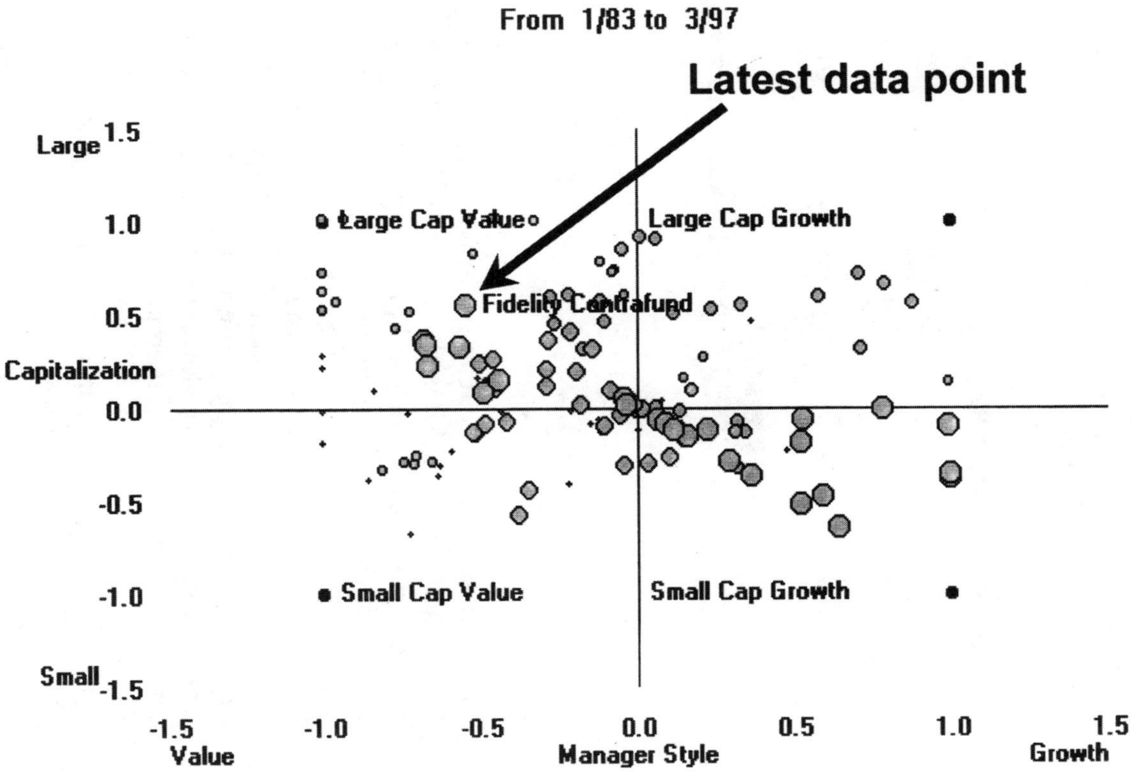

From 1/83 to 3/97

Source: Frontier Analytics, Inc.

FIGURE 8–15

Fidelity Contrafund: Returns Method Manager Analysis, Attribution
from January 1993 Forward

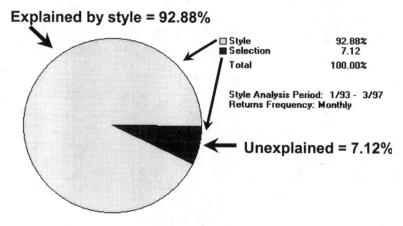

Explained by style = 92.88%

☐ Style	92.88%
■ Selection	7.12
Total	100.00%

Style Analysis Period: 1/93 - 3/97
Returns Frequency: Monthly

← Unexplained = 7.12%

Source: Frontier Analytics, Inc.

the smallest circle. The circles get progressively larger over
time. The latest point has the name of the fund near it,
which in this case is in the Large Cap Value quadrant.
Figures 8–13 and 8–14 show the controlled drift by Danoff
from small and mid-cap to large cap.

Next, let us *zoom in* to the period starting in 1994.
Figure 8–15 shows that style benchmarks explain 93 percent
of the returns of Contrafund. Figure 8–16[10] shows
Contrafund style history starting in 1994. The right side of
this chart shows the heavy emphasis on Large Cap Value.
Figure 8–17 shows the style map for the period. This chart
is not as cluttered as the last style map. With Figures 8–16
and 8–17 the drift to large cap is very clear.

---

10. See Figure 8–10 for definition of indices from Frank Russell Company.

FIGURE 8–16

Fidelity Contrafund: Returns Method Manager Analysis, Style History from January 1994 Forward

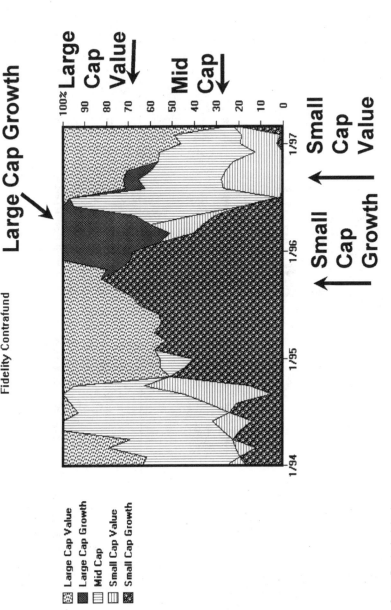

Fidelity Contrafund

Large Cap Growth

100% Large Cap Value

Mid Cap

Small Cap Growth

Small Cap Value

Large Cap Value
Large Cap Growth
Mid Cap
Small Cap Value
Small Cap Growth

Source: Frontier Analytics, Inc.

217

FIGURE 8-17

Fidelity Contrafund: Returns Method Manager Analysis, Style Map from January 1993 Forward

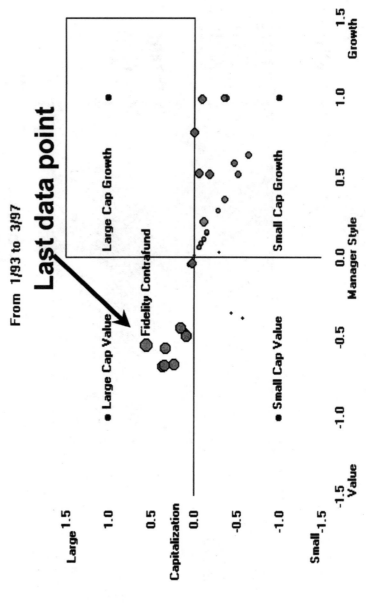

From 1/93 to 3/97

Last data point

Source: Frontier Analytics, Inc.

FIGURE 8–18

Fidelity Contrafund: Returns Method Manager Analysis, Cumulative
Excess Returns over Benchmark

Monthly Excess Compound Returns

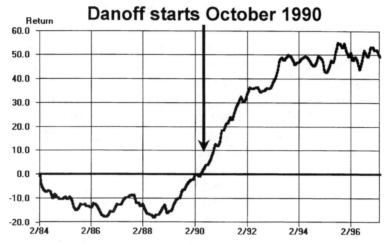

Source: Frontier Analytics, Inc.

Look at Figure 8–18. It shows the cumulative excess
return over the style benchmark using the returns method.
This is a calculation of the cumulative unexplained return
(Figure 8–15) over the style benchmark return. Danoff's
tenure started in October 1990. Notice that the curve moves
up nicely after Danoff took over. Starting in late 1993, however, the cumulative excess return curve levels off. The
cumulative excess return becomes essentially stagnant.
Danoff did not outperform his style benchmark going forward from 1993.

MPT statistics on Contrafund in Morningstar corrobo-
rates this information. It shows something interesting about

alpha, that is, return above expected return. The alpha for this fund, with the S&P 500 as the benchmark, is −1.3 percent for the last 3 years. Someone might say that a comparison with the S&P is not fair because Contrafund was historically a mid-cap fund. Yes, but lately Danoff changed the character of the portfolio to one where large company stocks make up the bulk of the market capitalization of the fund. At the end of 1993, the size of the fund was just over $6 billion. The transition began in 1994. By 1995 it was a large-cap fund. When you move to large cap, you have to face judgment as large cap. The Domestic Large Cap style class is perhaps the most intensely competitive on the planet. This is the segment with the most securities analysts that put stocks under the microscope. If ever there were an efficient market, this would be it. A glance at the record for 1994, 1995, and 1996 shows that Danoff underperformed the S&P 500 each year and by 564 basis points on average for the 3-year period ending April 1997. The 3-year Morningstar risk for this fund is 91 percent compared with a Vanguard Index 500 Morningstar risk of 70 percent. In other words, Danoff's management of risk is better than the average equity fund but not as good as an index fund in the same style class.

What is going on here? Would investors be better off with an index fund? This question is especially appropriate for those considering an initial purchase of this fund given the 3 percent front load. Perhaps this recent underperformance goes to an age-old discussion about fund size. Here are questions to ponder: At what level of assets under management does increasing size impair the ability of a manager to produce a superior record? Does this level differ for each manager? Is Danoff at that point or beyond it? Would the Contrafund shareholders be better off if this fund separated into two or more funds?

Here is a subtle point to consider. There are cases when the Morningstar *category* for a fund and the *style box designation* do not agree. That is the case with Fidelity Contrafund. As I write this, the category is *mid-cap blend*. The style box designation is *large-cap blend*. The style box reflects the fund positioning *as of the most recent portfolio*. The basis for the category assignment is *the past 3 years of style boxes*. If Danoff continues with large cap as the dominant strategy, you should expect the Morningstar category assignment to move there as well.

FIXED-INCOME FUND MANAGER ANALYSIS

Now let us shift gears. Look at Figure 8–19. This is the style box set for Fixed-Income Funds from Morningstar. On the

F I G U R E 8–19

Morningstar: Fixed-Income Style Box, Portfolio Method

Average Weighted Maturity or Duration

Credit Quality ↓	Short < 4Yr	Intermediate >= 4Yr, <= 10Yr	Long > 10Yr
High >= AA			
Medium <= AA-, >= BBB			
Low <= BBB-			

Data Source: Morningstar Principia.

left side, you see degrees of credit quality. Across the top is average weighted maturity.[11]

SCUDDER INCOME FUND

Let us apply manager analysis to Scudder Income Fund. The manager since 1986 has been William Hutchinson. Joining him as comanager in 1994 was Stephen Wohler. Hutchinson and Wohler like to add value by forecasting or anticipating the direction of interest rates and then adjusting the portfolio duration accordingly. Now look at Figure 8–20. This is the Morningstar style history of this fund using the portfolio method. There you can see a shift from *long-term*, high quality, to *intermediate term*, high quality.

Now look at a manager analysis using the returns method. Figure 8–21 is the set of benchmarks I used. They are all from Salomon Brothers.[12] I added 90-day treasury bills as cash equivalents to detect the degree that Hutchinson goes to the sidelines. Figure 8–22 shows that the style benchmarks explain 97 percent of the returns of this fund. Figures 8–23[13] and 8–24 show the style history and style map for this fund. There you can see the controlled drift from long term to intermediate term, high qual-

---

11. Morningstar makes an effort to convert this axis to duration, a more sophisticated measure of the interest rate sensitivity of a fund. Unfortunately, many fixed-income funds do not calculate this number or furnish it to investors.

12. "Copyright 1997 Salomon Brothers, Inc. This graph contains data from Salomon Brothers, Inc. Although the information in this graph was obtained from sources that Salomon Brothers, Inc. believes to be reliable, Salomon does not guarantee its accuracy, and such information may be incomplete or condensed. All figures included in this graph constitute Salomon's judgment as of the original publication date."

13. See Figure 8–21 for definitions of indices from Salomon Brothers, Inc.

Scudder Income Fund: Manager Analysis, Style History, Portfolio Method

Scudder Income
Release Date: 03-31-97

	EQ Style	FI Style High/Int	Objective Corp Bond--High Quali

Performance: Investment Style History

	1997	1996	1995	1994	1993	1992	1991	1990	1989
Total Return	-0.5	3.4	18.5	-4.5	12.7	6.7	17.3	8.3	12.8
Decile Rank Hybrid	-	-	-	-	-	-	-	-	-
% Stocks	-	0	0	0	0	0	0	0	0
% Bonds	-	84	96	89	91	94	96	93	96

Equity

	1997	1996	1995	1994	1993	1992	1991	1990	1989
Investment Style									
Average for Style	-	-	-	-	-	-	-	-	-
Decile Rank Style	-	-	-	-	-	-	-	-	-
Number of funds in Style	-	-	-	-	-	-	-	-	-
Style with Highest Returns									
Style with Lowest Returns									

Fixed-Income

	1997	1996	1995	1994	1993	1992	1991	1990	1989
Investment Style									
Average for Style	-0.50	5.41	16.48	-3.26	13.13	-	-	-	-
Decile Rank Style	7	6	3	-	-				
Number of funds in Style	1111	1013	938	58	1	-	-	-	-
Style with Highest Returns									
Style with Lowest Returns									

Source: Morningstar Principia.

FIGURE 8-21

Scudder Income Fund: Returns Method Manager Analysis, Benchmarks

Series	Style
Salomon Brothers Inc. Corporate 3-7 yrs.	Intermediate Corporate Bonds
Salomon Brothers Inc. Corporate 10+ yrs.	Long Corporate Bonds
Salomon Brothers Inc. Intermediate Hi Yield	Intermediate High Yield Bonds
Salomon Brothers Inc. Long Hi Yield	Long High Yield Bonds
3-mo T-bills	Cash Equivalents
Scudder Income Fund	Fund for analysis

Source: Frontier Analytics, Inc.
Data Source: Morningstar and Salomon Brothers, Inc.

FIGURE 8-22

Scudder Income Fund: Returns Method Manager Analysis, Attribution from July 1985 Forward

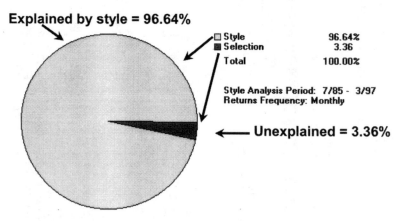

Explained by style = 96.64%

□ Style	96.64%
■ Selection	3.36
Total	100.00%

Style Analysis Period: 7/85 - 3/97
Returns Frequency: Monthly

⟵ **Unexplained = 3.36%**

Source: Frontier Analytics, Inc.
Data Source: Morningstar and Salomon Brothers, Inc.

Scudder Income Fund: Returns Method Manager Analysis, Style History from July 1986 Forward

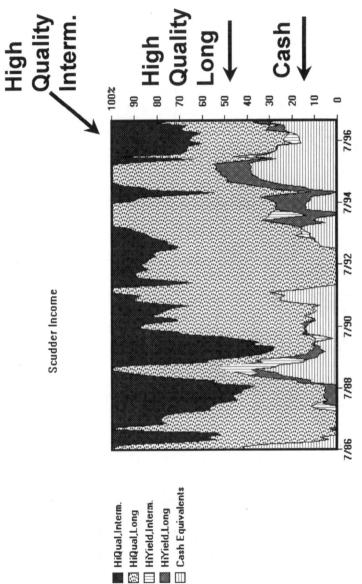

Scudder Income

High Quality Interm.

High Quality Long

Cash

HiQual.Interm.
HiQual.Long
HiYield.Interm.
HiYield.Long
Cash Equivalents

Source: Frontier Analytics, Inc.
Data Source: Morningstar and Salomon Brothers, Inc.

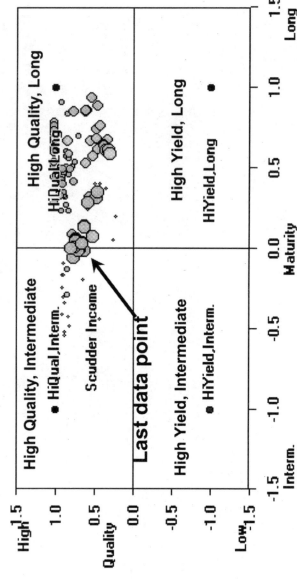

FIGURE 8–24

Scudder Income Fund: Returns Method Manager Analysis, Style Map from July 1986 Forward

Source: Frontier Analytics, Inc.
Data Source: Morningstar and Salomon Brothers, Inc.

ity. Morningstar shows that Hutchinson is roughly 15 percent in cash. Cash is the style class shown at the bottom of Figure 8–23. You can see that the model detected the cash content also.

What about this unexplained attribution of *only 3 percent?* This suggests that Hutchinson does not add much value. Look at Figure 8–25. The returns method shows that the cumulative excess unexplained return for the fund is negative, that is, less than the benchmark. What does Morningstar show? The fund has a negative alpha for 3-, 5-, and 10-year periods. Over a 10-year period, the fund underperformed the Lehman Brothers Aggregate Bond

FIGURE 8–25

Scudder Income Fund: Cumulative Excess Return over Benchmark, August 1986 Forward

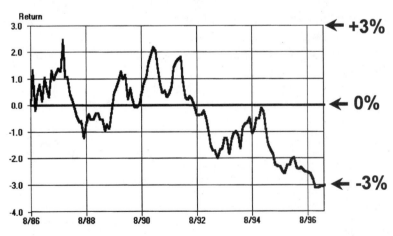

Source: Frontier Analytics, Inc.
Data Source: Morningstar and Salomon Brothers, Inc.

Index by an average of 24 basis points. Over the same 10 years, the fund underperformed the Lehman Brothers Corporate Bond Index by an average of 78 basis points. Where is the added value from active management?

MANAGER ANALYSIS USING THE RETURNS METHOD

My work shows that a *limited number* of funds do not lend themselves to manager analysis using the returns method. Returns-based analysis reveals a low correlation in spite of my best efforts to find a set of benchmarks that have an acceptable attribution level. When I encounter this, I often find that the manager does not neatly fit into any Morningstar style box either. I find this often with managers that use illiquid securities, restricted stock, convertibles, warrants, preferreds, derivatives, or other exotics. It may also simply raise a red flag suggesting that I should be extra cautious before committing client dollars to the fund. For example, try running a returns-based style analysis on Frontier Equity,[14] American Heritage, or Rydex Ursa. Good luck! As I write this, the Morningstar style boxes are *blank* for these three funds. The analysts at Morningstar could not find a foot to fit the glass slipper either.

Does this mean we should reject out of hand any manager that walks Frost's road "less traveled"?[15] No. We have

14. The Frontier Equity fund has an interesting profile to say the least. According to Morningstar, it has a front load of 8 percent. It has an expense ratio of 7.29 percent. Each year of the 5-year history shows a negative return. The average annual 5-year return is −14 percent. The assets under management are $1.2 million. The management fee is 1 percent, and the fund is open for new purchases!
15. "Choice" by Robert Frost.

to reach a decision using other evidence. Marty Whitman at Third Avenue Value is an example of a manager that must take Frost's poetry to heart. He does not fit the mold. Try a returns-based style analysis for him. Marty often likes to buy those companies taken by others for dead. He sees value that others miss. Roughly, 58 percent of his equity position is in financial stocks. Is it a sector fund? He likes inverse floaters.[16] (What? You don't know what they are? Neither did I. I had to look it up too.) He likes debt of those companies near or in bankruptcy. He views the efficient market hypothesis and Modern Portfolio Theory with scorn and derision. (I can tell because his body language is very demonstrative and his adjectives are very colorful on this topic.)

Morningstar puts him in the small-cap value box. As I write this, his portfolio is only 63 percent in stocks. Twenty-six percent of his portfolio is in cash. He sticks to his buy discipline. It is hard to find bargains just now. The Morningstar category for him is "domestic hybrid," that is, more that 30 percent of the portfolio is in something other than stocks. His turnover is only 14 percent, which translates into a holding period of 7 years. His 5-year return is 128 basis points above the S&P 500. His fund is on my buy list and has been for quite some time.

HOW TO FIND OUT MORE ABOUT MANAGER STYLE ANALYSIS

In addition to the illustrations shown in this book, other firms offer manager style analysis software. Listed below is the Web site for a representative sample of firms, and they

---

16. No, this is not a new baseball pitch.

can give you an overview of their products. The target audience for this software is the institutional client, the sophisticated investor, and their advisors. This is not a blanket recommendation for these products. Each has its strengths and weaknesses. You must try them out and decide if they are appropriate for your circumstances. Exclusion from this list does not imply that I considered and rejected any product or firm.

I recommend that you try out the returns method as another tool in the bag to see if it is right for you. As in the case of the geologist or the doctor, you must be prepared to read about it and work with it for several months to sharpen your skills. It takes time to become comfortable about what works and to learn about the limits of the technique. I hope that the information here shortens the learning curve for you. I also recommend that the highest and best use of this tool be as a *corroborating companion* to the portfolio method. *Exclusion of the portfolio method from your techniques is likely to obstruct your vision.* That is why I included the Morningstar Web site here.[17]

Company	Internet Address
BARRA	http://www.barra.com
Frank Russell Company	http://www.russell.com/
Ibbotson Associates	http://www.ibbotson.com
Morningstar, Inc.	http://www.morningstar.net/
Zephyr Associates, Inc.	http://www.styleadvisor.com/
Callan Associates, Inc.	http://www.callan.com/

17. There is no significance attributable to the proximity of Morningstar, Inc., and Ibbotson Associates in this list. (Just kidding.)

DO NOT OVERDO IT!

A word of caution seems appropriate. It is possible to shoot yourself in the foot and carry style investing too far. Dogmatic adherence to style investing can have the unintended result of eliminating very good managers with a blended or eclectic approach. Jean-Marie Eveillard at SoGen International and George Mairs III at Mairs & Power Growth are two examples. To include very good managers like this, I usually have a core-satellite approach to portfolio design. The core part of the portfolio has either multistyle managers or institutional asset class funds with low expenses. The choice between the two depends on the outcome of discussions with each client about the advantages and disadvantages of each approach. The satellite portion has the style-specific managers.

TO THE MANAGER: CAN WE TALK?

After I have narrowed my prospective buy list down to a manageable number, I then like to talk with the managers. I learn things in that setting that I would never know otherwise. There are several ways to encourage this interaction. Here is my list in order of preference:·

1. One to one
2. Small group
3. Over the phone
4. Seminar
5. Videoconference
6. Telephone conference

I find these sessions help me to *take a subjective measure of the manager.* I like to do this not only through *what they say* but also *how they come across.* You might prefer the term *body lan-*

guage. I make judgments about the manager concerning such items as *intellect, discipline,* and *the ability to articulate a strategy with clarity and conviction.*

QUESTIONS TO ASK

1. What is the overall investment philosophy of your firm?
2. What is your specific management style?
3. Have you changed your style over time?
4. What is your process for selecting securities?
5. How do you manage risk?
6. Is the focus of your strategy one of concentration or diversification?
7. Do you specialize in any particular sectors or themes?
8. What is your sell discipline?
9. Under what circumstances do you hold cash above a level required for redemptions?
10. If you expect a down market, what do you do about it?
11. What is the expense ratio of your fund?
12. How does that compare with your competitors?
13. What are the components of your expense ratio?
14. What role do you take in expense containment for the fund?
15. How do you manage the cost of turnover?
16. What approach do you employ to minimize the impact of taxes?
17. Do you use illiquid securities, restricted stocks, derivatives, margin, or short selling?

18. Do you expect to modify your strategy as your fund grows in size?

19. At what frequency do you release information about portfolio holdings?

20. Under what circumstances would you close your fund to new investors?

21. To what degree do you have your personal assets in the fund?

22. Does your firm retirement plan use your fund?

23. How are you compensated?

24. What other managers or investors out there have a style most like yours?

25. What is the profile of the investor most suited to buy your fund?

26. What is the single most important message we should take from this discussion?

Reprise

Let us take one more pass over the major themes of this book. This section is mostly for advisors, but clients and investors are welcome to read along also.

SETTING INVESTMENT POLICY

Preparing an Investment Policy Statement serves many purposes for your clients and for you:

    1. *Educational tool:* The process of developing and updating an IPS provides many opportunities for you to educate your client,   which is critical to your working relationship. I find that most clients come to the table with a certain amount of intellectual baggage about investing and investments. The process of putting the IPS in place and maintaining it with client participation allows you, the advisor, to address misconceptions and maintain proper focus.

    2. *Communications tool:* An IPS is a broad script that

you expect to follow on behalf of your client. With it, your clients will have a greater level of comfort about their investments. They will know what to expect. If you did a thorough job, they will even know what to expect when crunch time comes, the tide goes out, and the music stops. The IPS is also great to refresh memories, both yours and your clients', about what you planned to do with the portfolio and why you are doing it.

3. *Tailored to each client:* The IPS reflects the profile and unique needs of each client. It includes goals that are defined, quantified, prioritized, and placed on a timeline. It documents the client's degree of investment sophistication and understanding of investment risk and suitability. It includes any restrictions or limitations that your client and you want imposed on the portfolio. It helps you to fulfill your obligation as a fiduciary to your client.

4. *Working document:* The IPS is not a fancy binder that sits on a shelf somewhere gathering dust. It is a working document. The advisor and the client should refer to it on a regular basis. This is necessary to eliminate any confusion or ambiguity from a memory lapse. To stay on course, it is critical for the advisor to have the profile of the IPS firmly in mind as he or she manages the portfolio.

5. *Remains relevant:* The IPS process is a continuous one. There is a scheduled refresh of the document on a regular basis, and it serves to reaffirm the understanding between the advisor and the client. Typically, the frequency is annual. Immediate portfolio modification can be appropriate under certain conditions. There may be a significant change in client circumstances. There may be a material change in assumptions or the character of one or more asset classes before that scheduled review. If so, there is latitude and flexibility built into the process to adapt and modify the IPS when and as there is a need to do so.

6. *Enhances your image:* There is no doubt that a well-done IPS reflects favorably on advisor credibility in the eyes of the client. The use of an IPS is one aspect of professional performance that defines the line between very good and mediocre advisors. I think that I know which side of that line you want to be on.

A GOOD PLACE TO START:
THE ASSET CLASS LEVEL

Modern Portfolio Theory and its successors provide many benefits. It introduced the notion that each investment category, or asset class, has its unique profile of return and risk. Risk has several dimensions. The important idea is that it can be managed. You can do more about the management and control of risk than return. That comes about through an assemblage in a portfolio of several asset classes that have peaks and valleys at different times. Many providers offer software that optimizes portfolios using these techniques. Here is a warning flare: Please pay attention as I send it aloft.

The directions on the package read, "Pop it in the microwave for 3 minutes and you are ready to eat." The last 40 years have provided many extraordinary advances in portfolio design techniques. These have included advances in the scientific method and in state-of-the-art technology. Application system developers have spent a great deal of time making their software easy to use.

An environment like this can cause an advisor to fall into the trap of a canned, commoditylike approach to the client. Beware of complacency or of becoming intellectually brain dead about the portfolio design process.

Do not allow yourself to fall into the trap of thinking that the computer and the software are going to do all the work for you. In the first place, you have to put the results of each computer run through some reasonableness tests. In most cases, you still have to interpret the results. You cannot do this unless you understand what is going on under the hood. That takes many hours, months, even years of study and practice. There is still no substitute for training, hard work, and experience to add value to the process.

PASSIVE INVESTING

There is a favorite spectator sport at financial conferences for investment professionals. It is the inevitable slot on the program about passive-versus-active investing. Over the years, I find that these debates produce more heat than light. I believe that passive investing is a viable strategy. I use it in the core part of the portfolio for many clients.

My concern is the misinformation that is out there. There is a great deal of hype about *indexing.* Many make the mistake of using *indexing* and *passive investing* as synonymous terms. People who approach the subject of passive investing in this manner put the emPHAsis (sic) on the wrong sylLABle (sic). It is not about indexing. It is about return to the shareholder after fund expenses, transaction costs, and taxes. Many good actively managed mutual funds compete favorably with index funds on this field under these ground rules.

In addition, not all index funds are competitive. Some have high expenses. Some have high turnover. Some even charge a sales load!

There is still not much of a choice out there in the world of index funds. In raw numbers, there are only 127 index funds as I write this. About half of these focus on U.S. Large Cap Equities. That narrows the field in a material way for the other asset classes out there. Why are there so few? There are two obvious reasons.

1. *It is good for business:* Mutual fund providers follow the active-is-better premise for business reasons. Actively managed funds demand higher fee revenue from the shareholders.

2. *Lack of demand:* It has been only in the last few years that funds like the Vanguard Index 500 have become popular with shareholders. The style of this fund is *large-cap blend.* That is why you see so many other funds companies providing offerings in this category. They want in on the action. Until recently, there was also a lack of demand from advisors. Index funds representing other asset classes are a recent phenomenon. This is a response to the demand mostly from the advisor community.

Advisors and shareholders have to be vigilant about abusive fund expense ratios. Expense ratios come out of the pocket of the shareholder. They are a direct reduction from return. One can be sanguine about the expenses of a small fund. It takes certain minimum costs to operate a fund. As a fund grows in size, certain economies of scale should take hold. The expense ratios should go down. For most funds, that is the case. Unfortunately, there is abuse out there. For the abusers, the high expense ratios stay high or even go up. There is also abuse in the components of the expense ratio. Perhaps the most extreme is in the so-called 12b-1 fee. Through this fee, funds pass marketing and distribution costs on to the shareholder. Shareholders pay the fund for marketing to prospective shareholders and to handhold existing shareholders. Why should the shareholder bear this cost burden? Then there is the ultimate outrage. Some funds charge this fee although they are closed to new investors!

ACTIVE INVESTING

Let us suppose that you decide to select funds that employ active management. In doing this, you raise the bar. It is extraordinarily difficult to be successful at this task. Here are some of the obstacles in your path:

1. *Laws of large numbers:* It seems as if there are another thousand or so mutual funds added to the field every year. Today there are more than 8,000 names out there. I just said that there are only 127 index funds. The rest of the 8,000 are actively managed. The first task is to cut through that mountain of data to get to a list of *suspects.* Your database of mutual funds must be comprehensive, accurate, and timely. If any of these qualities are missing, you have lost the race before you even start.

2. *Odds are against you:* Unfortunately, the vast majority of funds out there have characteristics that are unappealing. Some pundits suggest that performance should have no bearing on manager selection. I think that this is an extreme position. I have much more confidence in a manager with a long-term record that is consistently in the top quartile versus a manager who is consistently in the bottom quartile. I do agree that a selection strategy based on performance in isolation is flawed. There are other important characteristics to consider. These include expense ratios, turnover, tax efficiency, concentration, composition, and manager style. The decision should also incorporate subjective considerations drawn from answers to questions put to the manager. This investigation takes time and effort. To do less exposes you to fund selections that are unsuitable for your client.

STYLE AND SUCCESS

I find that the best mutual fund managers typically follow a specific style of investing. They are also often long-term investors. They have the discipline to stick to the strategy that they know best and to adhere to that strategy over the long haul. I prefer that a manager stop buying if there are no suitable candidate securities matching the style of the manager. The manager may even temporarily close the fund to prevent dilution and to maintain the quality and character of the portfolio. Some pundits interpret any cash buildup as a style shift or even market timing. I suggest that you not automatically jump to this conclusion. Forcing the manager to buy when there are no suitable goods on the shelf is simply inappropriate in my view. Shifting styles to chase the latest theme or trend can also be hazardous to client wealth. Not many managers do this well.

As an advisor, you may design client portfolios at the investment category or asset class level. If this is the case, you want fund managers that maintain their style discipline. That way you can manage the asset class weighting consistent with the client portfolio design. If you choose managers that shift styles or strategies, you give up much of the control and management of the portfolio strategy.

So how do we determine manager style? One way is to look under the hood at the internals of the portfolio. Find out the characteristics of the security holdings. Some refer to this approach as the *portfolio method*. The data that you get from the prospectus or a reporting service like Morningstar are 6 to 12 months out of date. Even so, data that have gathered a little dust are far better than no data at all. This information is vital for the advisor to make an informed decision about a manager.

Another way to get a perspective about manager style is through use of the *returns method*. I find that a 6-month look-back period is the most useful. It makes the aging of the style data roughly the same as the portfolio method. This method is relatively new when compared with the portfolio method, and, in fact, it is still very much in evolution. I have worked with it for several months. Institutional investors use this technique frequently for evaluating money managers of institutional portfolios.

What about mutual funds? There are far more data available for mutual fund managers than for private money managers. Why then should we bother to learn and use the returns method for evaluating mutual fund manager style? Is the portfolio method not enough in the case of mutual funds? After more than 3 years of testing, I concluded that the mastery of the returns method is worth the effort. I find that it is most useful as a corroborating tool. Divergence between the portfolio method and the returns method for a given fund raises a red flag—it is a signal to dig deeper. If I encounter this for a fund, I do not buy it until I resolve this issue to my satisfaction.

THE END OF THE BEGINNING

To paraphrase Winston Churchill, this is the end of our journey—and perhaps the beginning of another. I hope that I get a chance to meet you in person some day. I would like to hear what you think about what I said here. For those of you who are advisors, I would like to know if I met my goal, which was to provide you with three or four ideas that you can use in your practice. I count only those ideas that improve the productivity of your client portfolios. For investors, I hope that there are useful ideas for you also. Please keep all this in perspective. Unlike Alice in Chapter 1, I suspect that you have at least a general idea about where your clients want to go. Unfortunately, there is no quick fix to get there. To help your clients reach their goals, there is usually no substitute for (1) having a plan, (2) doing your homework, and (3) applying a dose of common sense.

INDEX

About the Author

Ron Rutherford, MS, MBA, CFP, CIMA, is Chairman and CEO of Rutherford Asset Planning, Inc., a fee-only financial planning and investment consulting service based in New York City. He started the firm in 1986 after rising through the management ranks of IBM, managing strategic and financial planning activities for software products around the world. Consistently listed by *Worth* as one of the top financial advisors in the U.S., Rutherford has appeared to discuss financial topics on national television, including CNN, Headline News, CNNfn, and Fox News Network. The financial press regularly quotes his opinions. He has taught courses at The New School—Department of Finance and CFP-in-training courses at New York University. Rutherford is a member of a number of professional societies, including Investment Managers Consultants Association, National Association of Personal Financial Planners, and the Institute for Certified Financial Planners.